The Sponsorship Seeker's Toolkit

Anne-Marie Grey & Kim Skildum-Reid

The McGraw-Hill Companies, Inc.

Sydney New York San Francisco Auckland
Bangkok Bogotá Caracas Hong Kong
Kuala Lumpur Lisbon London Madrid
Mexico City Milan New Delhi San Juan
Seoul Singapore Taipei Toronto

McGraw·Hill Australia

A Division of The McGraw·Hill Companies

National Library of Australia Cataloguing-in-Publication data:

Skildum-Reid, Kim.
Sponsorship seeker's toolkit.

ISBN 0 07 470707 8.

1. Corporate sponsorship—Australia. 2. Promotion of special events—Australia. 3. Fundraising—Australia. I. Grey, Anne-Marie. II. Title.

658.152240994

Published in Australia by
McGraw-Hill Book Company Australia Pty Limited
4 Barcoo Street, Roseville NSW 2069, Australia
Acquisitions Editor: Kristen Baragwanath
Supervising Editor: Anna Crago
Editor: Carolyn Pike
Designer: Lara Scott
Illustrators: Alison Wallace, Alan Laver
Cartoonist: Hank Hero
Typeset by Post Pre-press Group
Printed in Hong Kong by Best Tri Colour Printers & Packagers Co. Ltd.

Forewords

Imagine a book that outlines the strategies, skills and tactics necessary to build strong, mutually beneficial relationships that benefit your business. *The Sponsorship Seeker's Toolkit* is for anyone looking to execute a marketing agenda that achieves specific business goals while raising funds—from sport and community events to government and especially non-profit organisations.

In many countries, the non-profit sector is rich in compassion and idealism but is dependent upon the excess funds that individuals, corporations and other organisations are willing and able to donate after their own needs are met. It is incumbent upon those of us working within non-profit organisations to not just work harder or raise more money but to fundamentally rethink how we achieve our mission and the structures we've put in place to do so.

Our response must be to commit ourselves not only to redistributing wealth but to creating a new kind of community wealth—resources generated through profitable enterprises to promote social change. Creating community wealth encompasses a number of activities, including cause-related marketing campaigns, business ventures, licensing agreements and sponsorship agreements.

Sponsorship is a way of creating wealth to serve the public interest. Now more than ever the non-profit sector needs to find new ways to raise revenue and become financially self-sustaining. Here lies the opportunity for non-profit organisations to learn new skills and techniques that will equip them to uncover new sources of revenue, achieving their social mission and generating new resources.

Sponsorship provides an opportunity for companies, individuals and businesses to achieve their goals while raising critical funds for non-profit organisations and their causes. This book outlines the skills necessary to utilise sponsorship opportunities successfully in order to achieve your financial, marketing and social goals. It is possible for a business to do well while doing good.

The Sponsorship Seeker's Toolkit serves as a roadmap for finding corporate sponsors—no more being lost, going in circles, or searching aimlessly. This guide tells you how to find them, how to get them and, most important, how to keep them. The steps outlined in this book will be of practical value to anyone who is working to improve their community. Sponsorship is a powerful strategy for creating new wealth but you need the skills to seize it.

William Shore
Executive Director
Share Our Strength
Washington, D.C. USA

I've often said that sponsorship is a little bit of science, a little bit of art and a little bit of magic. Of course, the reality today is that sponsorship is a whole lot of science before one can ever get to the art and magic part.

Sponsorship, as a medium, is exiting its adolescent period and entering its rightful place as a mature marketing discipline. Understanding the science of sponsorship is now a must for all marketing professionals.

My friends, Kim Skildum-Reid and Anne-Marie Grey, two of our industry's brightest young talents, have produced an outstanding body of work, *The Sponsorship Seeker's Toolkit*, focusing on the science of sponsorship. This 'how-to' workbook provides a valuable aid for the event manager and corporate sponsor alike.

For the beginner, this book provides a complete framework for understanding and leveraging sponsorship. And the sponsorship veteran will find dozens of insightful 'nuggets' of ideas to implement.

Rick Jones
Chief Executive Officer
Corporate Marketing Associates
Dallas, Texas USA

Contents

About the authors

Kim Skildum-Reid

Kim started her sponsorship career twelve years ago by crashing a sponsor's blimp into a high-power line and nearly blacking out the Houston Astrodome during a nationally televised football game. Luckily for her clients, it's been uphill from there!

Over seven years, she worked for numerous Fortune 500 clients in the United States on their sponsorships of blue chip properties as diverse as the Superbowl, US Open Golf and the International Chili Society Cook-Offs, as well as dozens of major professional sporting organisations and concert tours.

Kim moved to Australia in September 1992 and, in January 1994, she started her own consultancy specialising in corporate-side sponsorship strategy. Clients have included ANZ Bank, Australia Post, Optus Communications, Dunlop Tyres, Ansett Australia, Volvo, NEC, Peters Ice Cream, Toyota, Qantas, James Hardie, Canberra Milk, Orix Australia, George Weston Foods, ABN AMRO and Daewoo.

In October 1996, Kim started Smart Marketing Streetwise Workshops with Anne-Marie Grey. They now tour extensively, providing top-quality sponsorship workshops on a variety of subjects to both sponsors and sponsees.

In August 1997, Kim retired after four years as President of the Australasian Sponsorship Marketing Association, Inc., an organisation of which she was a founder. During her presidency, Kim led the growth of the organisation from thirty to one of the strongest and most active sponsorship associations in the world.

Kim is also a recognised speaker and author, with dozens of articles to her credit. She holds the prestigious position of sponsorship columnist for *Professional Marketing* magazine, Australia's largest circulation marketing publication.

Anne-Marie Grey

Anne-Marie Grey, Director of Grey O'Keefe and Associates, specialises in developing strategic alliances between cultural, sporting, non-profit associations and organisations and the private sector.

Since 1990, Grey O'Keefe and Associates has raised over $15 million dollars for cultural and non-profit organisations, including the National Gallery of Australia, the National Museum of Australia, the Australian War Memorial and the Australian Healthcare Association.

Anne-Marie's knowledge and understanding of cause-related marketing, cultural policy and funding issues have resulted in consultancies with the Australian Sports Commission, the Department of Communication and the Arts and the Institute of Aboriginal and Torres Strait Islander Studies.

Prior to establishing Grey O'Keefe and Associates, Anne-Marie was Manager, Marketing and Development, at the National Museum of Australia, with responsibility for establishing foundation sponsorship, program evaluation, marketing and revenue generating programs for the organisation. .

Anne-Marie worked with the National Gallery of Australia for five years before establishing Newman Grey and Associates, a professional strategic marketing consulting firm, that specialised in assisting cultural organisations with sponsorship, marketing and management advice.

Anne-Marie studied at Colby College in Maine, USA, holds undergraduate and graduate degrees in Art History from the Australian National University and has studied marketing and management at Monash Mt Eliza and the Graduate School of Management at the University of New South Wales. Anne-Marie is a member of the Fundraising Institute of Australia, the Public Relations Institute of Australia and former National Secretary of the Australasian Sponsorship Marketing Association.

Anne-Marie is presently developing corporate partnerships as Director, Creative Enterprises and Marketing, for Share Our Strength, one of America's leading organisations in the fight against hunger and poverty. Anne-Marie resides outside Washington, DC, with her husband, Kieran and two children.

Preface

Sponsorship is an investment in sport, the arts, a community event, individual, venue,
broadcast, institution, program or cause which yields a commercial return for the sponsor.

Sponsorship has existed in one form or another for centuries. Ancient athletes
competed not only for the love of their homeland but for the glory of the wealthy
sponsors who fed and housed them while they trained. For hundreds of years, artists
endeavoured to attract wealthy patrons, allowing them to live comfortably while the
patrons used the relationships to bolster their standing among their peers. And intrepid
explorers circled the globe in great sailing ships sponsored by royalty who wanted theirs
to be the flag flown by the heroes of the day.

Modern sponsorship, however, is a relatively recent occurrence. In the early 1980s,
only a handful of corporations were using event marketing, as it was called then. The
majority of sponsorship dollars were spent on advertising spot buys during televised

sporting events, and event signage gained popularity. Sports attracted almost all the money, with corporate expenditure in the arts or on causes still treated as philanthropy. Back then, sponsorship was measured in terms of impressions—one person seeing a logo one time is one impression—without much concern as to whether those people were in the sponsor's target market. Actually measuring shifts in customer behaviour or perceptions was extremely rare.

With the massive price rises in advertising rates throughout the 1980s, the advent of new delivery media, including cable television, as well as an increased consumer awareness and appreciation of sponsors, sponsorship became accepted as a new alternative marketing medium.

According to IEG, Inc. (see Appendix), by 1988 sponsorship was the fastest-growing form of media in North America. Sponsors were moving beyond seeing sponsorships as simply an opportunity for corporate entertainment and enhanced profile. Companies were using sponsorship as an interactive participatory platform for involving customers and building sales. Corporations' belief in sponsorship grew. They knew that it was contributing to their overall marketing success, but the true impact and potential of the medium remained a mystery.

Since then, sponsorship has grown increasingly sophisticated, objective-based and integrated with overall marketing programs. The results have been huge, with sponsors around the world finding that sponsorship, when done well, has a higher and more lasting impact on the perceptions and buying behaviour of their customers than any other marketing option. This is because sponsorship is a two-way medium. It creates a *relationship* between sponsors and their target markets. Sponsorship says to consumers that the sponsor understands them—that the sponsor cares about what they care about. Sponsorship has now finally come into its own as the most powerful of all marketing media.

According to IEG, Inc., in 1998, more than 4500 companies spent more than $6.8 billion dollars on sponsorship in North America. Worldwide spending is estimated to be $10 billion. And spending in Australia and New Zealand is estimated to be $660 million per year.

And it's not just elite sports any more. Sponsorship properties now range from the Olympic Games to local public schools, arts festivals to Federal government conferences, sports stadiums to the Internet. Elite athletes wear golden Nikes. The local milk authority sponsors a rugby team of nine-year-olds. The privileges of American Express membership include free entry to art museums. And for every can you buy, Pal dog food will make a donation to the Guide Dogs.

Because sponsorship has moved out of the realm of managing directors supporting their favourite football teams or museums and into the realm of achieving very real marketing objectives, your job as the sponsee has become even harder. You need to accept that sponsorship isn't about you any more. It's about what your sponsor needs, and they will sponsor whoever will provide them with the most cost-effective way to achieve their objectives. That means that you are not only competing with other organisations of the same type for sponsorship dollars, but are on an even footing with all sponsorship seekers, including sporting organisations, the arts, community events, celebrity endorsements, entertainment and sporting venues, and causes.

Sponsorship is about how much value you can provide to a corporate sponsor. It is important that both parties achieve their objectives and recognise that they have achieved something of value. That is the magic word that separates sponsorship from philanthropy—value. This book has been written to provide you with the expertise and tools you need to shift your focus and create that value for a potential sponsor.

We cannot guarantee that every proposal you present to a sponsor will be successful. Nor can we promise that all your sponsorship programs will be flawlessly executed. We can, however, assure you that the techniques, tools and templates included in this book will assist you in creating and maintaining strong, objective-oriented sponsorships. By following our step-by-step program, you will have a solid foundation on which to build highly innovative win—win partnerships.

Acknowledgments

We would like to acknowledge the following people and organisations for their assistance during the development and production of this book: Joy Window, Alison Kahler and Peter Hansen for getting us in front of the right people; William Shore and Rick Jones for gracing us with their wonderful forewords; Lionel Hogg for going above and beyond the call of duty with the agreement pro forma; Tony Burrett; Martyn Thomas for all of the media advice; all the folks at McGraw-Hill Australia; and whoever invented the Internet, without which this transcontinental writing project never would have happened.

We would particularly like to thank our families and friends for their patience, encouragement and support throughout the development of Smart Marketing Streetwise Workshops, and especially the writing of this book.

Most of all, we would like to thank all of the people who have attended our workshops all over the world. We appreciate your openness about the challenges you face, and we appreciate all of your input, allowing us continually to improve our skills. Without you, this book would not have been possible.

And finally, a special thanks to Edward for motivating us to achieve more than we ever thought possible.

How to use this book

There are a lot of people who think creating sponsorship requires some kind of mystical, magic power. We're here to tell you that as surely as the beautiful assistant doesn't really get sawed in half, there is no magic behind developing strong, lasting and mutually beneficial partnerships with sponsors.

We fully believe that building and maintaining these partnerships can be achieved by people with little or no sponsorship experience, so long as they have two things: enthusiasm and a roadmap. The enthusiasm you will have to supply yourself but this book is your roadmap.

We suggest using the book as follows:

➤ Read through the book once first, taking notes as you go. This will help you to understand the desired outcome when you start to implement the strategies that we have outlined.

➤ Ensure that key stakeholders within your organisation know what you are doing (reading the book themselves may help). The system we advocate is a big departure from the approach many organisations are currently taking to sponsorship—you need to ensure you have support for the change.

➤ Check out the resources we have outlined in the Appendix. Start increasing your knowledge level right away.

➤ Go through the book, doing the exercises outlined along the way. Don't get hung up on the formats. The ones we have used are what works for us, but feel free to alter them so that they work for you.

➤ Use the exercises collaboratively whenever possible. There are a number of places where two or more heads are definitely better than one.

➤ Be proactive with potential sponsors. The assumption is often that, because they have the money, they know what they are doing. This is often not the case at all. Once you have completed this book, you may very well know more about doing sponsorship right than they do, and it may be an educational process for them, too.

➤ Have fun with it. Good sponsorship is a highly creative process. If you don't allow yourself to have big, creative, sometimes silly ideas, you'll never hit upon the really great ones.

Special notes

Throughout this book, we will often generically use the word 'event' to describe the property for which you are seeking sponsorship, whether that is an event, venue, cause, organisation, program, individual or team. Also, if you don't understand a term, be sure to check out the glossary of terms in Appendix 1.

If you don't understand a term, check the glossary on page 164.

Overview of sections

The book is broken into four general sections. Below is an overview of what is included in each of them.

Part 1—Planning

In this section, you will look closely at both your event and your organisation to determine what you need to plan and implement a sponsorship program effectively. Long before the selling process begins, you need to determine whether you and your organisation are prepared to engage in long-term relationships with the corporate sector. We will guide you through creating internal policies, undertaking market and corporate research, creating a marketing plan and negotiating promotional media.

Part 2—Sales

In this section, you will learn about preparation and persistence. Both are required to guide your proposals successfully through to the negotiation stage. This section shows you how to identify potential sponsors, research them, create a customised proposal for every potential sponsor and negotiate a mutually beneficial deal. Included to assist you are a number of detailed checklists and forms, as well as a sponsorship proposal template.

Part 3—Servicing

This section outlines how to create and implement innovative sponsorship servicing programs that ensure your partnerships are win—win for all parties concerned. Covered are steps that will get your relationship off on the right foot, quantification and reporting mechanisms, and a wide range of maximisation options, which will assist your sponsors in achieving all they can from their investments.

Part 4—Appendix

It is essential that you continue to develop your sponsorship and marketing skills and build up your resources. To this end, we have included a listing of resources, including associations, Internet sites and publications that will assist you in creating and developing a sponsorship portfolio that will bring your organisation and your sponsors the results you desire. Also included is a comprehensive glossary of terms and an outstanding Sponsorship Agreement Pro Forma template, provided by one of Australia's foremost experts on sponsorship law.

Part 1

planning

Chapter 1

Internal planning

Before your organisation begins the sponsorship acquisition process, it is essential to consider your organisation's ability to enter wholeheartedly into a marketing partnership with a corporation. Too many organisations turn to sponsorship as a last minute resort for raising much-needed funds. Sponsorship, however, is no longer a fundraising activity but, rather, a joint marketing activity involving both your organisation and a corporate partner. If you are not prepared to be part of a win–win partnership and share ownership of your programs, your sponsorship efforts will fail. You may be successful in raising sponsorship, but retaining your sponsors will be very difficult.

Also, it is important that everyone within your organisation understands that sponsorship is about creating win–win partnerships between your organisation and a corporate sponsor. If the sponsorship is to succeed, you need to fulfil both partners' marketing objectives. This shift from fundraising and corporate philanthropy to marketing-driven sponsorship programs is the major point of difference from sponsorship programs in the 1970s and 1980s and sponsorship in the new millennium.

Often the most difficult challenge for a sponsorship manager is changing the attitudes of staff within the organisation from a fundraising perspective to a marketing perspective. The majority of organisations who seek sponsorship do so from a position of need—the need for funds is continual and ever pressing. Many organisations are concerned that corporate partnerships and sponsorship will threaten their credibility and integrity. However, from a corporate perspective, sponsorship is a marketing activity.

And this is just the tip of the iceberg. In fact, there are often several hurdles that you will need to overcome in order to gain the support of your staff and Board.

Some typical areas of concern with sponsorship include:
- being seen as 'going commercial'
- implied perceived ownership of an organisation or event
- selling out to the corporate sector
- compromising the integrity of programs and services
- placing financial objectives before programming objectives

Sponsorship is a joint marketing activity, not simply a method for raising funds.

➤ allocation of much-needed resources to marketing activities

➤ placing consumer needs ahead of staff needs

➤ lack of recognition as to the value of sponsorship to the organisation

➤ refusal to deal with particular industries or specific companies

➤ 'Government should fund this program and we should not be seen to be absolving them from their responsibility.'

➤ 'We tried it before and it didn't work.'

As a sponsorship manager, you will need to determine what the critical issues of concern are within your organisation and devise strategies to deal with them. Interviews with staff throughout your organisation, as well as interviews and surveys with Board members, clients and customers are efficient methods for determining the critical issues of concern. Many of these issues may not appear to be legitimate to you. However, perceptions and issues are always real, even if they are not accurate. You will need to address these perceptions none-the-less.

Often you will need to lead your questioning in order to pull out the specific area of concern or the exact nature of the issue. Reluctance to engage or support sponsorship activities is often highly emotive. Exercise great care, compassion and consideration in your interviews.

We should acknowledge that most sporting organisations have long held a commercial outlook on sponsorship. If you are in the sporting area, you will probably have a much easier time garnering internal support for your activities. This does not make you immune from internal dissension and questioning, particularly if you are expanding your sponsorship program to include grassroots or community service activities.

Once you have determined what issues are relevant to your planned sponsorship programs, you are better able to develop and implement strategies to confront them or to take corrective action.

Creating a sponsorship-friendly organisation

In order to develop a sponsorship-friendly organisation, we recommend a multipronged approach:

➤ stay in contact with your staff and Board

➤ educate all internal stakeholders

➤ provide reports, case studies and so on to all staff

➤ create a sponsorship team.

There are often several hurdles to overcome in order to gain staff support.

Sporting organisations are not immune to staff dissension on sponsorship.

Stay in contact

Just as you need to keep in close and constant contact with your sponsors, you also need to communicate continually with your staff, members and Board. You want to cultivate an appreciation of sponsorship marketing principles and create an organisation that will fully maximise every partnership.

Educate staff

We have found that conducting staff workshops, explaining sponsorship marketing principles and organisational approaches to sponsorship, is an effective strategy for engaging staff in a sponsorship program. Regular presentations to the Board outlining policies, strategies and results are not only effective but also politically wise.

Report results to all staff

Regular case studies, progress reports and interviews with sponsors should be included in all staff communications. Remember to involve all staff, not just marketing and public relations people, in your communications program.

Create a team

Creating a sponsorship team of decision makers from across departments and outside resources is a great step in creating a shared sense of responsibility for sponsorship across your organisation.

Monthly meetings with your sponsorship team are almost guaranteed to provide you with additional opportunities for building a commitment to sponsorship within your organisation, while maximising your sponsorships and minimising your costs. For the investment of a couple of hours and a tray full of sandwiches, you will gain insight into many untapped resources and unearth potential trouble spots that could cause problems further down the track. Most importantly, though, you will gain the support, co-operation and understanding that it takes to create a fantastic sponsorship program.

When putting together your team, remember not to overwhelm the group with 'marketing people'. The point is to create a multifaceted think tank. Consider including representatives from the following areas:

➤   advertising agency
➤   media partners
➤   corporate communications
➤   customer service

- employee representation
- market research
- merchandising
- tourism
- packaging/production
- product management
- public relations
- membership
- ticket and group sales
- concession sales
- sales promotion
- sponsorship consultants.

Remember to keep the team up to date on all developments throughout the process—
a one- or two-page update a couple of weeks after each meeting should be adequate.

Planning your sponsorship programs

As is the case with any successful program, outstanding sponsorship programs require
thorough research, careful planning and flawless execution. There are two critical
strategic planning documents that should be the linchpin of your sponsorship activities:
a sponsorship policy and a sponsorship strategy. Both documents dovetail with your
organisation's mission statement and business plan. See Figure 1.1.

Sponsorship policy

Find out if your organisation has a sponsorship policy in place. If there is, ensure it is
updated to reflect your current situation. If not, start developing one as a matter of urgency.
   A sponsorship policy is a necessity for every organisation seeking sponsorship, even
traditional sponsorship seekers such as sporting groups. It is one of the most often
overlooked components of a sponsorship program despite compelling reasons for
having one. For example:

- Any program generating or distributing substantial funds should define the
  principal objectives and administrative processes of the sponsorship program.
- A sponsorship policy will ensure that your organisation has a uniform approach
  to sponsorship.

Figure 1.1
Internal planning process

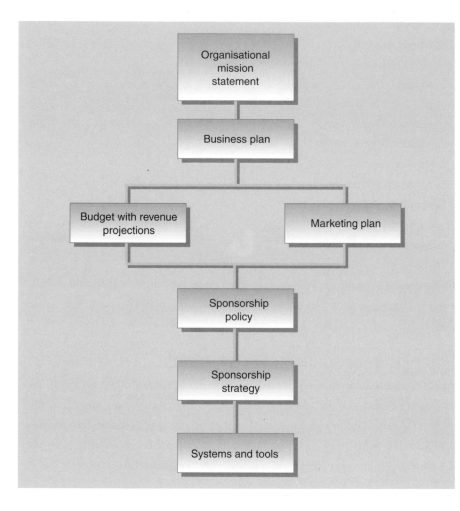

> A policy outlines accountability and responsibility. This point is particularly important if your organisation is in receipt of government funds or enjoys non-profit status.
> A policy outlines specific issues that are relevant to your organisation's approach to sponsorship and will detail exclusions and limitations.

Components of a sponsorship policy

A sponsorship policy should contain certain information. This is outlined below.

Background

The background outlines the history of sponsorship within your organisation, as well as your organisation's approach to sponsorship.

Definitions

The definitions state what does and does not constitute sponsorship (this is particularly important if you receive government funding and/or philanthropic donations). They also define the internal stakeholders in the sponsorship program.

Situational analysis

The situational analysis identifies all current issues that may impact on your sponsorship program.

Exclusions

The exclusions section clarifies and describes fully what companies and industry sectors you will not engage with in a partnership arrangement.

EXAMPLE

In Australia, Commonwealth government legislation prohibits tobacco companies from engaging in sponsorship marketing partnerships. Also, many organisations that work with children will not enter partnership agreements with companies producing alcoholic beverages.

For each exclusion, provide a rationale as to why a partnership with this company or industry sector is unacceptable. You may find over time that the issues prohibiting partnerships are no longer valid. You will also be prepared to answer questions from the Board and members of the public as to why partnerships with these companies are unacceptable.

Processes and procedures

The processes and procedures that your department will use to secure sponsorship agreements and manage your sponsorship programs are specified here.

EXAMPLE

If your sponsorship acquisition process is to be centralised, explain why. Outline the processes by which you will follow up sponsorship leads or provide comments and progress reports to the senior management, financial management and auditors. If you are an organisation with a national office and state branches, describe how information and leads will be shared and benefits negotiated across the organisation as a whole.

This section will describe how you are actually going to manage the sponsorship acquisition program and service your sponsors.

Delegations

Delegations describe who within your organisation is delegated to sell, receive and approve sponsorships, and to what dollar level.

Many organisations are required to have Board approvals on delegations related to the distribution of organisational information and financial transactions. Preapproved delegations can certainly make the audit process smoother for everyone involved.

Approvals and contracts

This section explains who can approve a sponsorship and clarifies when a contract is required.

Accountability and responsibility

Accountability and responsibility describes who within your organisation is responsible for your sponsorship programs. Responsibilities will include seeking and reporting sponsorship funds, processing, banking and investing funds and servicing sponsorship relationships.

Review and evaluation

Review and evaluation defines when the policy will be reviewed and evaluated. Review your policy no less than every six months. Publicise the results of the review process and encourage input from staff and members.

ENSURE THAT YOU INVOLVE YOUR CEO

Frequently asked questions about sponsorship policy

Who should create the sponsorship policy?

If your aim is to create a policy that your staff and members feel they own, involve as many of the staff and members as possible.

Some smart sponsorship managers create a draft policy after discussions with staff, sponsors and members and then present the draft policy to staff for comment. Other managers form a working party to thrash out the draft document. Whatever method you choose, ensure that you involve your chief executive officer, as well as your financial and human resources managers. Without their backing, your policy is not going anywhere. Finally, you will want to have your policy formally accepted by your Board.

Alternatively, secure the services of a sponsorship consultant to guide your organisation through this process. Sometimes, it can be easier and far more effective to have a consultant do the work for you. Ensure that the consultant works closely with your organisational stakeholders or the organisation will have no sense of ownership for the policy.

How long should the policy be?

Your sponsorship policy should be as long as is required to outline your organisation's sponsorship principles, processes and accountability procedures. Some sponsorship policies are as short as two pages, while others are closer to ten pages.

Is a sponsorship policy necessary? Shouldn't I be concentrating on getting the money in and not worrying about documenting processes and systems?

Non-profit organisations, in particular, are under increasing scrutiny from their Boards, their members, the media, auditors and government departments as to their source of funds. The time you invest in creating and documenting your guidelines, systems and processes is never wasted. A policy, endorsed by your Board, ensures that your organisation is credible, legitimate and strategic. You have a responsibility to your stakeholders to ensure that your processes and accounting procedures are as transparent as possible. Taking the time to plan and document today may save you a lot of time and heartache in the future.

How do you motivate staff to create a policy?

Staff in your organisation may have been through many of these exercises previously. How do you motivate them to go through one more of these planning sessions?

If the issue is important to them, they will participate. You need to listen carefully to what issues are of concern and be prepared to engage in a relevant discussion of their issues. The bottom line is increased revenue and marketing muscle for your organisation. Staff might not be particularly interested in how you get it but they are bound to have ideas on how to distribute the funds. Find the nerve point and work from there.

Sponsorship policy questionnaire

Go through the sponsorship policy questionnaire below to ensure you have covered all issues. At the end of this process you should be ready to draft your sponsorship policy. Take the time to consult as widely as possible before drafting your policy.

List the key stakeholders that will be affected by this policy and then ensure you speak with a representative from each stakeholder group. Include staff and union representatives, marketing and public relations staff, front of house staff, sales staff, finance and resource officers, auditors, Board members and senior staff. Also include program staff and recipients of sponsorship funds, along with members of your organisation if appropriate.

Background

➤ Why does our organisation want to engage in sponsorship?

➤ Do we see sponsorship as a fundraising exercise or a marketing activity?

➤ Do we want to develop long-term win–win partnerships?

➤ What are the overall principles of our approach to sponsorship?

Definitions

➤ How does our organisation define sponsorship?

➤ How does this differ from philanthropy and/or government support?

➤ Who are the internal stakeholders? (Board, sponsorship department, marketing department, etc.)

Situational analysis

➤ How many people are currently engaged in seeking sponsorship for the organisation?

➤ Is this our only responsibility or are we responsible for several other major activities?

➤ Where does the sponsorship office fit into the organisational structure?

➤ To whom do we report and how frequently?

➤ What resources are presently allocated to the sponsorship department? Are the funds sufficient?

➤ What training and professional development is available to the sponsorship department?

➤ Have there been any changes to the organisational structure or staff changes that impact on the department?

➤ Are there any political issues that affect our programs?

➤ How does our business strategy or organisational plan affect the sponsorship?

➤ Does our organisational culture embrace sponsorship and win–win partnerships or does work need to be done in this area?

➤ What issues will affect our sponsorship program?

➤ What issues do staff and our Board need to be aware of?

Exclusions

➤ What companies and industries do we refuse to work with in a partnership? List each company or industry sector and provide a detailed rationale as to why they appear on the exclusion list. Indicate when you will review or repeal this decision.

If corporate responsibility is important to your organisation (e.g. you run an environmental education program), consult ethical investment firms and the investment area of your bank to get up-to-date information on companies with socially and environmentally responsible values.

Processes and procedures

➤ What are our organisation's principles guiding the selling of sponsorships?

➤ How will we ensure sponsorship does not influence tendering processes (in the case of government and non-profit organisations)?

➤ How will we manage sales rights within our purchasing processes?

➤ How will we ensure that a sponsor does not exert control over our organisation or sponsored event?

➤ How will we protect and maintain our organisation's integrity and credibility?

➤ How will we value in-kind or contra sponsorships?

➤ How will we keep staff and other departments or sponsors informed?

➤ How will we train staff?

➤ How often will we report to the Board and to staff?

➤ How will we evaluate sponsorships for our organisation and for our sponsors?

➤ What procedures are in place for:

- selling sponsorship?

- ensuring all funds are accounted for?

- distributing funds?

- determining what projects will attract sponsorship?

- ensuring public interest is best served?

- acquitting sponsorship funds?

- maintaining and servicing sponsors?

- reporting on the program to Board, members and staff?

- handling inquiries from auditors, accountants, taxation officials, media and the general public?

➤ How will we handle a controversial sponsorship?

Delegations

➤ Has our resource management section ensured that the relevant financial delegations are in place for receiving, selling and approving sponsorships? State the specific delegations and approvals within the policy.

Accountability and responsibility

Who is responsible for:

➤ selling sponsorship?

➤ ensuring all funds are accounted for?

➤ distributing funds?

➤ determining what projects will attract sponsorship?

➤ ensuring public interest is best served?

➤ acquitting sponsorship funds?

➤ maintaining and servicing sponsors?

➤ reporting on the program to Board, members and staff?

➤ handling inquiries from auditors, accountants, taxation officials, media and the general public?

Approvals and contracts

➤ Who determines what benefits are available to potential sponsors?

➤ How is this determined?

➤ How often do we review our benefits list?

➤ Who can negotiate a sponsorship deal?

➤ Who can approve a sponsorship?

➤ What is the process for approving sponsorships?

➤ Who can sign final contracts?

➤ Will we use a letter of agreement or a contract?

➤ When will we consult a lawyer?

Review and evaluation

➤ When and how often will this policy be reviewed?

➤ Who will be involved in the review process?

➤ How will we review this policy?

➤ How will we communicate the policy amendments to our stakeholders?

Sponsorship strategy

Your sponsorship strategy is, very simply, the process that you will take to gain and retain sponsorship, and the attitude you take with every aspect of your sponsorship program.

The bulk of this book is about sponsorship strategy. When you finish the book and all of the exercises in it, you will have developed an approach—a personalised system that works for you. Document it—this is your sponsorship strategy.

Chapter 2

Marketing plan

If you want to succeed in your quest for sponsorship funds and strong sponsor relationships, you must ensure that you have access to people with the relevant marketing skills, sufficient resources, a good strategic plan, a marketing plan, market research information and a commitment to applying that market research.

Your organisation must be able to demonstrate to potential sponsors that it can capture and retain its audiences. Your products and services must be based on genuine market needs and values as opposed to what your staff think your clients want or what your organisation thinks its clients need.

As part of your organisation's strategic planning process, you will need to create a marketing plan. This is not a plan for marketing the sponsorships but rather is a plan for marketing your organisation and its events or products. In the case of an event or a property, every marketing plan must have a media plan, a publicity plan and an evaluation plan to measure performance. Every marketing plan must be based on audience market research as it needs to reflect your audience profile, the number of people who will attend your event and your ability to reach out and speak with your audiences. Developing your marketing plan will help you to determine what makes your organisation valuable to sponsors.

This chapter will take you through a series of worksheets, many in a question-and-answer format, that will assist you in completing the marketing plan template found at the end of the chapter. Tip sheets and checklists are scattered throughout the worksheets to assist you in your planning.

> Every marketing plan will have its base in market research.

> Realistically, no event will appeal to everyone.

Defining your target markets

It is often a temptation to define your target market as a 'general audience'—you *want* everyone to come to your event and you are sure that if they do they will enjoy themselves. You may even receive government funding or a grant that tells you that your event/organisation or whatever has to serve the whole community.

REALISTICALLY, NO EVENT WILL APPEAL TO EVERYONE

Unfortunately, in a marketing sense, virtually no organisation has the money or other resources to reach the entire marketplace effectively. The job, then, becomes how to determine and prioritise your target markets so that you maximise the effectiveness of your marketing program.

Your target markets are determined by two general criteria:

1. **Demographics.** This is the hard data about a person or marketplace, such as age, sex, marital status, whether they have children, where they live, income and employment status, as well as more specific information, such as whether they own a computer, how old their car is, how often they travel on business, etc.

2. **Psychographics.** This is the softer data on your market and relates to why people do what they do, what motivates them to prefer one product to another, lifestyle questions, etc. Examples of words used to describe a marketplace psychographically include 'active', 'value-for-money oriented', 'quality oriented', 'feminist', 'risk taker', 'strong environmental responsibility', 'macho', 'saver' and 'adrenalin junkie'.

A target market is a group of people with very similar demographic and psychographic profiles. You will probably have several target markets, some of which will be very different from each other. All of your target markets put together are called your audience. Try not to confuse these terms, as the distinction will become very important when it comes time to targeting potential sponsors.

There are also two types of target market:

1. **End users.** These are the people we normally consider as customers—the people who come to the event or venue, buy tickets or use your service. These

> Target markets must be defined both demographically and psychographically.

All of your target markets put together are called your 'target audience'.

people could also be exhibitors, in the case of an expo, show, or convention, or event participants, such as runners registering for a marathon. The **Target Market Exercise** below will help you to prioritise these markets.

2. **Intermediary markets.** Intermediary markets are the organisations that the end user will go through or take the advice of in order to participate. These are many and varied but could include:

(a) ticket sellers

(b) exhibition space sellers

(c) venues

(d) retailers (e.g. 'get your entry form at Foot Locker')

(e) convention and visitor bureaus

(f) schools

(g) reviewers

(h) public transportation and/or parking facilities.

The importance of intermediary markets will vary from one event to another. If you have a large number of intermediary markets, it may be useful to prioritise them using the target market exercise below.

Target market exercise

We have found the following exercise useful in enabling identification and prioritising of the target markets that make up your audience.

Step 1

Try to imagine that the entire marketplace is represented by the graph shown in Figure 2.1. You will see three things:

1. There is a certain percentage of people who will always come to your event—they just need to know when and where it is and they will be there.

2. There is also a certain percentage of people who will never come, no matter what you do.

3. The people in the middle—the people who can be convinced—are your opportunity. This is still a lot of people, though, so it needs to be assessed and prioritised.

Some of these people can be convinced relatively easily. It makes sense that it is most cost-effective to address your marketing activities to this group first. The less likely people are to come, the more difficult and expensive it will be to market to them. You may choose not to market to people who probably won't be convinced at all.

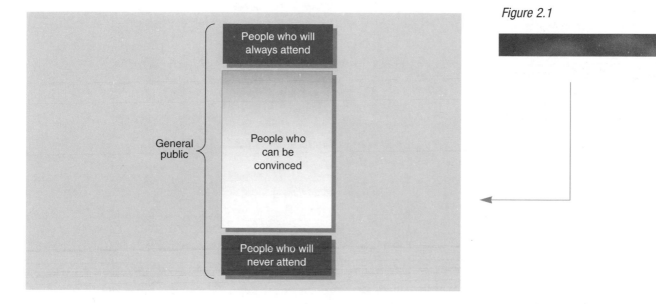

Figure 2.1

Step 2

Imagine that the 'always' group is already at your event and that the first one hundred people in your local telephone book are in a room. They each have a sign around their neck that shows all of their demographic and psychographic information (it's a really big sign!). It will cost you $1 each to speak to ten of them to convince them that they should go to your event. Who would they be? Describe them both demographically and psychographically—be detailed. This is your 'primary market'.

Step 3

Congratulations, those ten have been convinced and they are off enjoying themselves at your event. Now you can talk to another ten but they will cost you $2 each. Who would they be? Describe them both demographically and psychographically. This is your 'secondary market'.

Step 4

Keep doing this until you reach a point where you either run out of money or you determine that your marketing efforts will probably be very expensive for the return, in terms of participants. Usually, you will hit this point somewhere between three and five markets. This is your 'tertiary market'.

Figure 2.2 Prioritising your markets based on relative costs

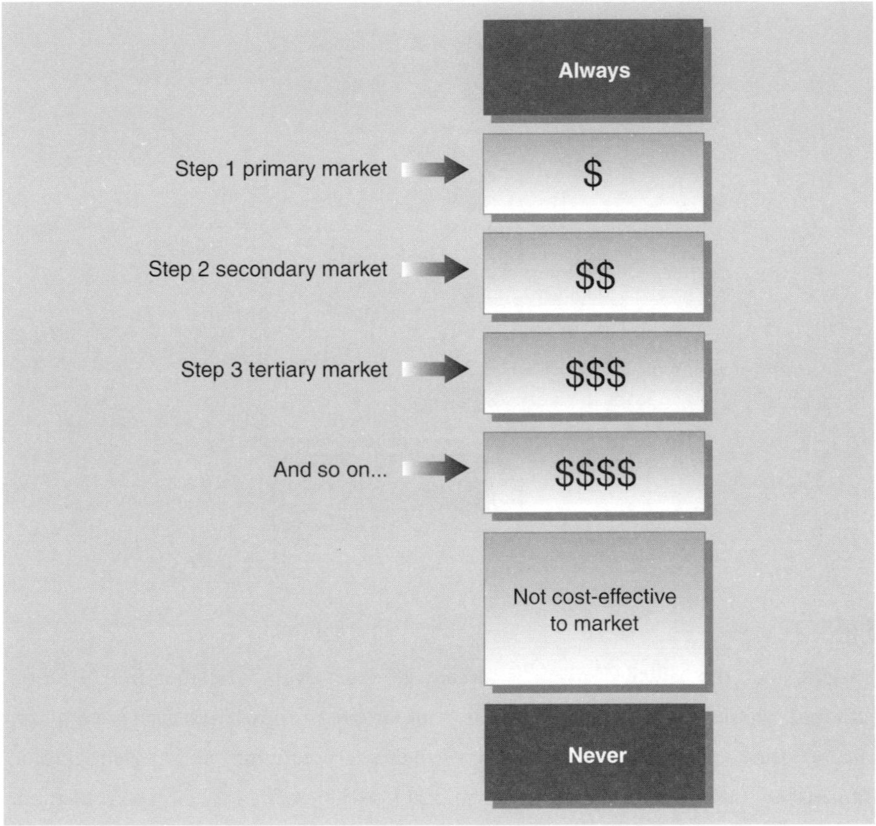

The goal is that, over time, your 'always' group will grow by pulling in some of the people in your primary and secondary markets as they become what we call 'true believers'. This will allow you to invest in the tertiary markets, expanding your audience year by year.

Target market assessment worksheet

Once you have defined your target markets, you need to assess them against a number of criteria. You should complete an assessment worksheet for your end users. If you have intermediary markets, you should complete a separate worksheet for them.

1. Clearly define your target markets (take this from research and/or your completion of the target market exercise).

    ....

    ....

2. What is the size of each of these markets?

    ....

    ....

3. How fast are these markets growing? What is the potential for growth in these markets?

    ....

    ....

4. Do geography or other logistical issues affect your product's or event's appeal to any of these markets?

    ....

    ....

5. Looking at your existing audience, who are the most important customers for your event or product? (This may be based on size, profitability to your organisation or other predetermined factors.) Rank your existing customers in order of importance to your event or product.

    ....

    ....

6. Who are all your potential customers in the market?

    ....

    ....

7. Categorise your existing and potential customers into segmented groups based on needs, motivations and demographic and psychographic characteristics. Completing the target market exercise may assist you in defining these groups.

    ....

    ....

    ....

8. What are the principal reasons why different customer groups attend your events, in order of priority?

....

....

9. What is important to your customers? (Think in terms of time, value, price, quality.)

....

....

10. What do your customers want? (Think in terms of benefits and needs. For example, your customers may have small children that need to be cared for at your event. As a benefit, you need to consider childcare or supervised children's activities.)

....

....

11. What are the five key things from a customer's point of view that you must do right to succeed? These are your critical success factors.

....

....

12. What methods will most effectively reach your existing and potential customer groups?

....

....

Once you have completed these questions and analysed your customer markets in depth, you should have a more complete understanding of your current and potential customers. Create a summary of your answers for inclusion in your **Marketing Plan Template** under the Target audience subheading.

Researching your target markets

You need to know a lot about your audience in order to reach them effectively. The best way to gather that type of data is very simple—ask them.

The benefits of conducting comprehensive research and truly understanding your markets are twofold.

1. **Marketing plan.** The research will give you not only an understanding of who your audience is but also of what motivates the different segments of it. This will

enable you to create a marketing plan that will reach them effectively and at the lowest possible cost because you won't be paying to reach people who are not in your catchment groups.

2. **Targeting sponsors.** The most powerful thing you can deliver a sponsor is your audience. Thus, it follows that the better you know your audience, the stronger your bond with your audience and the more desirable that bond will be to a sponsor. This will help you to target your sponsors more effectively.

What do you need to know?

When conducting research of your market you will need to ask a number of specific questions to obtain the type of information you will need to know. The questions you ask may relate to information from current customers and potential customers on their:

➤ age
➤ marital status
➤ income
➤ number and ages of children
➤ occupation
➤ recreational activities and preferences
➤ education
➤ car ownership—age of car, make and model
➤ postcode/zipcode
➤ mail order buying
➤ length of time at and present address
➤ travel and vacation preferences
➤ Internet use
➤ television viewing preferences
➤ club, organisation and affiliation memberships
➤ religion
➤ community involvement
➤ public transportation use
➤ purchasing habits
➤ disabilities
➤ fitness levels
➤ fashion consciousness
➤ state of health

> ➤ Frequent Flyer membership
> ➤ pet ownership
> ➤ sports enthusiasm
> ➤ interest in gardening or do-it-yourself activities
> ➤ political activity
> ➤ movie- or theatre-going habits
> ➤ home ownership
> ➤ interest in the arts
> ➤ beverage preferences
> ➤ food preferences.

Remember that information on product usage, propensity to buy and sponsorship attitudes may greatly assist your sponsorship sales process. If you can demonstrate that your customers actively seek out a sponsor's product, a potential sponsor is likely to be far more interested in you. If you approach a car manufacturer with research on the average age of your customers' cars, their car purchasing habits and their attitudes towards the car manufacturer, your potential sponsor is far more likely to consider your proposal seriously.

Primary and secondary sources

So, how do you get all of that information about your target markets so that you can create the strongest possible marketing plan? There are two main sources—primary and secondary. We will look at each separately.

Before conducting your research, you must understand that it will require an investment of time, money, or both. Once you have decided what information you are seeking, be sure to create a strategy and budget to achieve your research goals.

Primary information

As we stated earlier, if you want information about your target markets, ask them. Your potential audience is the best possible source for information about what will appeal to them and what kind of marketing will interest them enough to bring them to your event. This is primary information.

Primary information can be obtained by conducting: interviews with participants (such as runners in a 10 km race), attendees and potential attendees; surveys, including mail and telephone surveys, entrance and exit surveys, sponsorship awareness surveys, customer satisfaction surveys and focus groups.

Develop a strategy and budget for your research program, as the task can be both time consuming and expensive.

If you want information about your target market, ask them.

Sponsorship awareness surveys

Sponsorship awareness surveys are a useful tool for determining your customers' attitudes towards sponsorship in general and your organisation's sponsors in particular. Sponsorship awareness surveys can be done before, during or after an event to measure recall, retention of specific marketing messages and propensity to buy a sponsor's product.

Entrance and exit surveys

Entrance and exit surveys are used to gather demographic and psychographic data, and to measure awareness, unaided recall and promotional and advertising impact.

Focus groups

Focus groups are a highly effective method for gaining qualitative information on target markets and they are really easy and inexpensive to do. They involve getting together a group of ten to eighteen people who are representative of your target audience and asking them a range of questions about their opinions, preferences and lifestyles. If you do embark upon a program of focus groups, be sure to enlist an experienced moderator and preplan all questions to ensure you find out everything you need to know.

Interviews

Conducting a series of interviews with competitors, peers, industry specialists and individual customers is a valuable way of gathering primary information on your markets.

How to get primary information

A well-executed survey program need not be expensive. One of the cheapest ways to gather information is to utilise the services of a class at a business school or university. As part of their studies they need the opportunity to gather and analyse data, as well as presenting it, and you can provide that opportunity. The key here is not to treat them like research slaves but to work with them on both the methodology and reporting of results.

Another very inexpensive way to gather information is to run a simple drawing for a prize, asking pertinent questions on the entry form. This can work well but you will miss a whole segment of your market that is not motivated by that type of activity.

Templates for a Demographic and Psychographic Survey and a Sponsorship Awareness Questionnaire can be found on pages 25 and 27.

Contact your local
university and
college marketing
and advertising
departments.
Often there are
students
interested in a
market research
project.

Secondary information

Secondary information is any information that you get about your audience that does not come directly from your audience.

If you are trying to define your target markets and will not have the opportunity to research your audience directly, secondary information is the only way you will be able to gain an understanding of your markets. Secondary information can include information from:

➤ sponsorship, marketing or advertising publications and reports
➤ business information resources
➤ government bodies
➤ industry bodies.

Where to get secondary information

Many secondary resources are available that can be a gold mine of information for defining your target markets. In the Appendix of this book you will find a detailed list of resources, including associations, organisations and Web sites that will be useful sources of market information. Below, we have overviewed a few types of information resources.

Sponsorship, marketing and advertising

Getting market information from a sponsorship, marketing or advertising source is probably the user-friendliest way to get it. By its very nature, it will be marketing-oriented, offering some direction as to how to reach your target markets. These resources can include:

➤ professional associations
➤ publications
➤ reports
➤ media guides
➤ sports or arts governing bodies
➤ local or state special events office (some cities/states have them, some don't).

Government sources

Government sources are many and varied and mostly free. Contact your local reference library, state or Federal publications area and/or Census department to find out what is available. Many governments also publish lists of the available publications on the Internet. The type of government reports you could use include:

➤ American Statistical Index
➤ Australian Bureau of Statistics publications
➤ US Industry Outlook
➤ Census.

Business information sources

Depending upon what type of markets you are targeting, business information sources can be very useful for gaining market information. They are also good for obtaining background information on potential sponsors:

➤ *Who's Who of Business*
➤ Standard and Poor's industry surveys
➤ Hoover's on-line *Business Periodicals Index*
➤ *Statistical Reference Index*
➤ Dun and Bradstreet products.

Industry sources

Industry sources can also be very useful, particularly if your event or organisation targets primarily businesses and businesspeople. Such sources include:

➤ trade, industry, and professional associations
➤ Chambers of Commerce.

Sponsor awareness questionnaire

Research1.doc

Here is an example of a questionnaire that could be carried out on supporters of Basketball Canberra to determine how aware they are of the sponsors and, hence, how effective the sponsorship program is.

Basketball Canberra Club Registration Days—March 1998

Name the major sponsors of the Canberra Milk Quit Capitals.

....

....

I would be more likely to buy a product made by or use the services of a company that sponsors Basketball Canberra.

❐ Agree

❐ Agree somewhat

❐ Neutral

❐ Disagree somewhat

❐ Disagree strongly

When I see products made by companies who sponsor and support Basketball Canberra, I am more likely to purchase their products.

❐ Agree

❐ Agree somewhat

❐ Neutral

❐ Disagree somewhat

❐ Disagree strongly

When I see products made by companies that don't support Basketball Canberra, I am less likely to purchase their products.

❐ Agree

❐ Agree somewhat

❐ Neutral

❐ Disagree somewhat

❐ Disagree strongly

Are you a smoker?   ❐ Yes   ❐ No

Does anyone in your family smoke?   ❐ Yes   ❐ No

Would you like information about getting assistance with quitting smoking (e.g. Quit Courses, Quit Hotline), or receiving Quit information via mail?   ❐ Yes   ❐ No

Do you drink milk?   ❐ Yes   ❐ No

If Yes, which of the following products do you drink?

❐ Moove   ❐ Shape   ❐ Lite White   ❐ Canberra Gold   ❐ Canberra Milk

❐ Canberra Skim   ❐ Canberra Hi Lo

How much milk do you drink every day?

....

Why do you drink milk?

....

If you don't drink milk, why not?

....

What are the health benefits of including milk in your diet?

....

What radio station do you most often listen to?

....

What television station do you watch most often?

....

Demographic and psychographic survey

Research2.doc

Here is an example of a survey that could be carried out on people who have just attended the Woolloomooloo Theatre to determine the demographic and psychographic features of the target market.

We are carrying out a survey of visitors to Woolloomooloo Theatre. It will take about 10 minutes. May I ask you a few questions?

1. Is this your first visit to the Woolloomooloo Theatre?

....

2. How many times have you visited [if no]?

....

3. What show did you come to see at the Theatre today?

....

4. Where did you hear about the show? Check all that apply:

- ❏ friends and relatives
- ❏ tourist information centre
- ❏ tourist brochure, maps
- ❏ posters
- ❏ driving past
- ❏ another venue
- ❏ editorial commentary (please specify)
- ❏ television
- ❏ radio
- ❏ press
- ❏ magazine
- ❏ other (please specify)

5. What did you think of the Theatre?

....

6. What did you think of the show?

....

7. Did you come to the Theatre alone or with other people?

....

8. Including yourself, how many people are in your group today?

....

9. And are you here with:

- ❏ another family adult?
- ❏ a child/children?
- ❏ a non-family adult?
- ❏ an organised group?
- ❏ a school group?

10. Do you live in Sydney?

....

11. What is your postcode?

....

Non-Sydney residents only

12. How long are you staying in Sydney?

....

13. Are you staying in paid accommodation?

....

14. What other attractions have you visited/plan to visit during your stay in Sydney?

....

15. Are you a member of any other museum or gallery?

....

16. If you think of things that you can do with your free time, when was the last time, if ever, you did the following? (Circle appropriate response.)

	IN PAST WEEK	1–4 WEEKS AGO	1–6 MONTHS AGO	OVER 6 MONTHS AGO	NEVER OR DON'T KNOW
Go to the movies	1	2	3	4	5
Attend the first grade of a professional sporting event	1	2	3	4	5
Play sport or do an exercise program	1	2	3	4	5
Eat out at a restaurant	1	2	3	4	5
Go to a concert or play	1	2	3	4	5
Garden or work around the yard	1	2	3	4	5
Visit a museum, art gallery or exhibition	1	2	3	4	5
Go to the beach	1	2	3	4	5

17. For each of the following statements, please tell me if you agree or disagree that it describes you personally. (Circle the appropriate response.)

	AGREE	DISAGREE	DON'T KNOW
I am very fashion conscious	1	2	3
I want to achieve a lot	1	2	3
I am really a homebody	1	2	3
I hate getting dressed up	1	2	3
I like to garden and potter around the house on weekends	1	2	3
I would rather watch television on Saturday than go out	1	2	3
I thrive on the company of other people	1	2	3
I do not like sport, either watching or taking part in it	1	2	3
I would rather have a barbecue with friends than eat at a restaurant	1	2	3

18. Are you employed in paid work? What is your occupation?

....

19. Which of these age groups do you fall into? (Circle appropriate response.)

Under 18 years	1
18–24 years	2
25–34 years	3
35–49 years	4
50+ years	5

20. What is your highest formal qualification? (Circle appropriate response.)

Primary school	1
High school	2
Trade/technical or business college	3
Diploma	4
University degree	5
Other	6

21. Which of these categories best describes your household income? (Circle appropriate answer.)

Under $10 000	1
$10 000–$20 000	2
$20 001–$40 000	3
$40 001–$60 000	4
$60 001–$80 000	5
$80 001–$100 000	6
$100 001+	7

22. How likely are you to visit the Woolloomooloo Theatre again in the next 12 months? (Circle appropriate answer.)

Very likely	1
Somewhat likely	2
Not very likely	3
Not at all likely	4
Don't know	5

Thank you for your help.

Record sex: Female 1   Male 2

Date of interview: ....

I certify that this interview was conducted in accordance with the briefing instructions and that the information gathered is true and accurate.

Signed: ....

Developing the marketing plan

Now that you understand who your audience is, it is time to create a plan that will bring them to your event, venue, organisation or service.

SWOT analysis

SWOT stands for **S**trengths, **W**eaknesses, **O**pportunities and **T**hreats. The SWOT analysis is a tool that allows you to identify the internal and external issues that may impact on your ability to market your event or product.

Strengths and weaknesses are generally issues within your organisation's control.

Strengths and weaknesses

In order to identify the strengths and weaknesses of your event or products, you must examine the issues *within* your organisation that impact on your ability to sell your event or property to your target markets and to sponsors.

An important area to explore is how your organisation perceives the value of the event or product. If your organisation sees your event as a priority and an opportunity to raise the profile of the organisation, the event is considered a strength. However, if your Board sees your event as a drain on resources, then the event is a weakness.

EXERCISE

Consider the following list of internal organisational factors and determine how these will affect the success of your event. For each factor, determine whether its effect is a strength or a weakness and place your specific factors under either the strengths or weaknesses headings in the **SWOT Analysis Worksheet** found on page 35.

The internal factors that may influence your event include:

➢ staff attitudes and opinions

➢ staff experience

➢ the organisation's track record in staging and promoting similar events

➢ booster clubs, membership programs, databases

➢ how your corporate plan and your corporate objectives impact on your event

➢ key stakeholder analysis

➢ resources—money, people, assets, facilities, volunteers

➢ existing media profile

> media partners
> new organisational initiatives
> Board and/or head office support
> your location.

Opportunities and threats

The next step is to analyse all factors *outside* your organisation that may affect your event. The external analysis will assist you in identifying the opportunities and threats related to your event. Once having determined the threats to your event, you can then reassess the situation and analyse how you can make these threats into opportunities.

For example, if you are holding an outdoor children's community festival, the following external factors may influence your event:

> weather
> major sporting finals on the same day
> poor attendance at last year's event
> fewer number of children in the relevant age group in your community.

EXERCISE

Look at the following list of external factors that may influence your event and consider how these offer opportunities and threats to your event. Place your specific factors under either the opportunities or threats headings in the **SWOT Analysis Worksheet** found on page 35. Keep in mind that threats can often be turned into opportunities.

The external factors that may affect your event may be:

> political
> environmental
> geographic
> demographic
> historical
> industrial
> international
> local
> competitor related
> customer perception related
> economic
> consumer confidence related

Every threat provides an opportunity.

> technological
> legal
> natural.

Generally, threats are beyond the control of your organisation. You can anticipate and even plan for them but there is little you can actually do to stop them happening.

EXERCISE

Look at the list of threats you have compiled in the **SWOT Analysis Worksheet** (page 35). Determine which of these threats require your attention. What do you need to do in order to maximise or minimise the effects of each factor?

It is imperative that you address each threat to your event when conducting your planning to ensure the success of your event. Each threat can be further categorised into one of four types of threat to help you determine its importance to your event's success. Categorising the threat determines how you will respond to the threat to minimise its effect.

1. **Monitor.** Threats that you decide to monitor only are those for which there is little that you can do to change or plan for but for which you want to know what is happening. Examples might include any low-risk threats.

2. **Monitor and analysis.** Those threats that you decide to monitor and analyse are also ones that you can do little for to reduce but for which you need to determine how they might impact on your event.

3. **Contingency strategies.** Threats that you decide to prepare a contingency strategy for are those for which you can reduce the impact with planning. For example, if bad weather is a threat to your outdoor event, you can determine how you will handle it—postpone the event, move to an indoor facility or take out insurance.

4. **In-depth analysis and strategy development.** Those threats for which you decide to prepare an in-depth analysis and strategy development are those that have the greatest likelihood of impacting on your event. Technological, competitor and legislative factors are examples of threats that may require more detailed analysis and strategy development.

SWOT Analysis Worksheet

Strengths

Weaknesses

Opportunities

Threats

You are competing for your audience with anything they could do with their leisure time or money.

Competitor analysis

As with any company, you have competitors. It used to be that events only really competed for their audience against other events but, as more leisure options have come into play and leisure time has become more limited, this is no longer the case. In fact, you are competing against anything that a potential customer could do with their leisure time and money.

Use the following worksheet to analyse your competition.

1. Who are my direct competitors?

....

....

2. Who are my indirect competitors (television, movies, beach, etc.)?

....

....

3. What do my potential and existing customers like about my competitors' events, products and services?

....

....

4. How does my product or service differ from my competitors' products and services? (This is your unique selling point!)

....

....

5. How much are customers paying for my competitors' products or services?

....
....
....

6. What makes my competitors successful and why? What are they doing right?

....
....
....

7. How do my competitors communicate with their customers?

....
....

8. How do my competitors position their products and services within the market?

....
....

9. Who are my least successful competitors and why? What are they doing wrong?

....
....

10. What are my competitors' major strengths and weaknesses?

....
....

11. Are my competitors implementing any changes to their fees, products, marketing programs or operations?

....
....

12. Who are my potential competitors in the short- and long-term?

....
....

Marketing strategies

Now that you have completed your SWOT analysis and you know who your competition is, it's time to plan your marketing strategy.

In order to ensure your marketing strategy remains on track, you need to include the following information:

➤ objectives

➤ rationale for each objective

➤ strategies for achieving each objective

➤ quantification mechanisms to determine the outcome of each objective.

Objectives

Your objectives indicate what you want to achieve. They should be SMART objectives:

Specific

Measurable

Achievable

Results-oriented

Time-bound.

For example, if your stated objective is to obtain media coverage of your event, you have not been specific enough. Try, instead, 'to obtain a major article in *The Daily Express* and two major news stories on Channel 8 News and Radio Station 9CN by the second week of the festival'.

Rationale

The rationale must be a brief statement outlining why a particular objective or strategy has been chosen.

Strategies

Strategies indicate how you will meet an objective. Strategies are the specific actions that will be undertaken to achieve a desired outcome.

Quantification mechanisms

Quantification mechanisms are ways in which you will determine whether you have achieved your objectives and your customers' critical success factors. Quantification mechanisms may include, but are not limited to:

- sales figures
- sales growth
- quallty of medla coverage
- number of attendees
- customer opinion and satisfaction
- sponsorship awareness rates
- propensity to buy data
- reports
- number of events held
- number of sponsors
- number of new names for databases
- sales leads
- profit or revenue
- advance ticket sales
- wholesale ticket sales
- number and quality of cross-promotions
- customer propensity to return to the next event.

Sample

Objective

To obtain a major article with a colour photo in *The Daily Express,* as well as two major news stories on Channel 8 News and Radio Station 9CN during the second week of the festival.

Rationale

This will achieve an 80 per cent market penetration in our target markets and will give an added boost to ticket sales beyond the opening week rush.

Strategies

➤ Create a media kit for distribution to local media representatives.

➤ Create media interview opportunities with celebrity festival guests.

➤ Provide beta video tapes of last year's event and highlights of the first week to local television stations for ease of coverage.

Quantification mechanism

➤ Quality and acceptance of media kit.

➤ Number of media interviews.

➤ Number of broadcasts that utilise video tapes.

Strategies worksheet

As you start working out your objectives and how you will achieve them, this exercise may help you to understand the process behind their development.

1. What are my marketing objectives? For the purposes of this exercise limit yourself to no more than five objectives.

2. Provide a brief rationale for each objective.

3. For each objective, provide specific steps or strategies that you will undertake to meet the objective.

4. Record the relevant quantification mechanisms for each objective.

Sample worksheet

Complete this sample worksheet to develop your marketing plan.

Objective one

....

....

....

Rationale

....

....

....

....

Strategies

➤

➤

➤

➤

➤

Quantification mechanisms

➤

➤

➤

➤

➤

Remember to keep your objectives SMART—Specific, Measurable, Achievable, Results-oriented and Time-bound.

| Resources

All plans require resources. The resources required to implement your plan might include information, time, advertising expertise, graphic design skills, media talent, equipment, office space and staff, as well as funds.

In many cases, your marketing and promotional plans will be designed with a specific budget in mind.

Ask yourself the following questions to ensure you have addressed all your resource requirements.

1. What resources do you need to implement the marketing strategies? Sponsors can often provide non-monetary resources to a project. These should be clearly identified in your marketing plan.

2. How much funding do you require for these items? Include the number of hours, space required, training and administration support when budgeting for resources. Some examples include:

   (a) staff time (include overtime)   (b) printing

   (c) advertising   (d) distribution

   (e) equipment   (f) volunteer costs

   (g) office space   (h) travel

   (i) maintenance and storage.

3. What sources of information, data, knowledge, and research do you need? Remember to consider reports, in-house experience, surveys and consultant studies that already exist within your organisation. No one needs to reinvent the wheel.

Develop an action list

Having a plan does not mean anything unless you put it into action. These points are designed to enable you to create a master timeline and action list for your marketing plan.

1. Phase the strategies and timeline for each and every strategy. Ensure that each strategy has specific start and stop dates.

2. Identify who will be responsible for each step of every strategy.

3. Determine how each strategy will be evaluated, measured and reported. Identify who will be responsible for these tasks. Schedule all evaluations, approvals, meetings and reports into your master timeline and action list.

Marketing plan template

 *Market1.doc*

This template can be used to develop your own marketing plan. In the worksheets in this chapter you have been asked key questions and should have answered them comprehensively. If you haven't, go back to these worksheets and your research and do so now. Summarise and transfer this information by answering the questions in this template to develop your marketing plan.

Background

Why are we preparing this document? What do we want this document to achieve?

Target audiences

Who are we trying to reach? What do we know about them?

Critical success factors

What are the key things we need to achieve in order for this plan to be a success?

Market research

What are our strategies based on? (Summarise your research in dot points.)

Internal analysis

What within my organisation can affect this plan, both positively and negatively?

Environmental analysis

What factors in my environment can affect my purpose? What changes must we plan for? (State the assumptions you are making about the future.)

Competitor analysis

Who are our competitors?

Marketing SWOT analysis

What factors are hindering or restraining our purpose? What environmental factors are driving or assisting our purpose? (List here your strengths, weaknesses, opportunities and threats.)

Marketing objectives

Where do we want to go?

Marketing strategies

How are we going to get there? (Put these in dot points underneath your objectives; follow the sample on page 44.)

Evaluation

How will we know that we have achieved our objective? (Indicate how you will evaluate, measure and report against your key quantification mechanisms.)

Master timetable and action list

When will we get there? (Complete the following table to assist you in your planning.)

STRATEGY	TIME FRAME	ACTION OFFICER
Objective 1: (provide details)		
Strategy 1 detail	Start and completion date	Person responsible
Strategy 2 detail	Start and completion date	Person responsible
Strategy 3 detail	Start and completion date	Person responsible
Objective 2: (provide details)		
Strategy 1 detail	Start and completion date	Person responsible
Strategy 2 detail	Start and completion date	Person responsible
Strategy 3 detail	Start and completion date	Person responsible

Calculating overheads

When calculating your staff costs, you need to take into account your additional overheads. Adding these to the salary or hourly rate will give you the 'real cost' of employment.

You have two choices for calculating these costs. One is to calculate actual costs for all overheads (rent, equipment, utilities, insurance, etc.) and divide these by the number of staff and their hours. This is very time consuming and generally unnecessary.

The other option is to use a standard multiplier on salary or hourly rates. Most companies that approach real costs of employment this way use a multiplier between 1.4 and 2.6. In our example, we have used 1.9, meaning that if an activity will take an employee paid $10 per hour 100 hours to complete, the real cost of those hours will be $1900.

Resources

How much is it going to cost us to get there? (The following sample may be used as a format to assist your planning.)

Objective 1: Research current customers

STRATEGY 1

Survey subscription ticket holders to determine sponsorship attitudes and awareness levels.

Needs

$3500	Survey forms
$2000	Development of database (software, hardware upgrade)
$900	Contract researcher (20 hours @ $45 per hour)
$1710	Processor (40 hours @ $22.50 per hour plus overheads @ x 1.9)
$8110	Total for Strategy 1

STRATEGY 2

Survey users of Web site services and information.

Needs

$2500	. Post survey form on Web site and remove at conclusion of survey (outside of current contract)
$428	Processor (10 hours @ $22.50 plus overheads @ x 1.9)
$2928	Total for Strategy 2
$11 038	Total cost to achieve Objective 1

Follow this format for all objectives until you have costed all aspects of fulfilling your marketing objectives.

Review the marketing plan

Now that your plan is complete, you need to look back on it to double check that you have covered all of the key aspects.

Consider the following questions as you review your marketing plan.

➤ Do you have a clear vision of what the completed marketing campaign will look like?

➤ Have you identified the critical success factors and quantification mechanisms?

➤ Have you identified the key elements that need to be organised within your master timetable and action plan?

➤ Have you clearly identified all resources, including financial, human and training, that need to be planned for?

➤ Do you have a contingency strategy if parts of the plan don't work? Have you addressed all possible threats to your plan and event?

➤ Have you identified internal communication strategies within your plan? How will you report on progress to staff, members and your Board?

Continually reassess

A marketing plan is a living document. Ensure that you have scheduled review periods into your plan so that you can fine tune your plan throughout the implementation phase.

Chapter 3

Implementing the marketing plan

You have written your marketing plan and it's looking good. Now we need to make that plan work for you.

Although there may be a number of other aspects to implementing your marketing plan, the most common components are:

➤ media promotion
➤ publicity
➤ database/loyalty marketing
➤ signage
➤ the Internet.

We have included information about each of these components.

Media promotion

Although you can go out and simply purchase media, like any other company, this is not all that common, primarily because it ignores the fact that you have a lot to offer a potential media partner. Instead, most sponsees embark upon media promotion to achieve their objectives without spending a fortune.

Generally, media promotions are created with one or more media partners. You provide them with co-ownership of the promotion and either a paid schedule or sponsorship of your event (and all ensuing benefits), and they provide several times that investment in media value. This can be an extremely cost-effective way for you to get your message out into the marketplace.

Who should create the promotion?

Generally speaking, the sponsee is much more likely to achieve its goals if it is intrinsically involved in creating the promotion. See the **Nine Steps of Promotional Media** (page 49) for some hints.

Do you go to one or more media outlets?

If you have determined that you can achieve your objectives with either of two competing media outlets, our suggestion is that you brief them both on the promotion and ask them both to come back to you with a package that meets the brief.

If you have determined that there is only one media outlet that will suit your needs perfectly, you should negotiate closely with them to create a partnership. Do not let them hold you to ransom—you can always walk away and rethink your approach for a different type of media.

How much value should you get?

If your proposal is structured correctly (see the **Nine Steps of Promotional Media** on page 49), you should be receiving substantially more value from the media partner than the funds you invest. This is usually expressed as a value-to-cost ratio.

The table below outlines some value-to-cost ratios and what that value includes.

MEDIA	TARGET VALUE-TO-COST RATIO	VALUE INCLUDES:
Television	3:1 to 8:1	Paid spots
		Bonus spots (confirmed)
		Bonus spots (space available)
		Promotional spots (co-branded by the television station)
		News coverage
		Other editorial coverage (lifestyle, sporting or news magazine programs)
		Advertising production
		Use of on-air personality for endorsement, appearances, voice-overs or as a spokesperson
Radio	3:1 to 10:1	Paid spots
		Bonus spots (confirmed)

(Cont.)

MEDIA	TARGET VALUE-TO-COST RATIO	VALUE INCLUDES:
		Bonus spots (space available)
		Pre-recorded promotional spots (co-branded by the television station)
		Live promotional spots
		Live liners (very short promotional spots)
		News coverage
		On-air interviews
		Remote broadcasts
		Advertising production
		Use of on-air personality for endorsement, appearances, voice-overs or as a spokesperson
Newspaper	3:1 to 8:1	Paid advertising
		Bonus advertising (confirmed)
		Bonus advertising (space available)
		Insertion of program, poster or other promotional material that you supply
		Printing and/or design of program or poster
		Special supplement (can often be used as the official program)
		Advertorial coverage
Magazine	2:1 to 5:1	Paid advertising
		Bonus advertising (confirmed)
		Bonus advertising (space available)
		Special section
		Insertion of program, poster or other promotional material
		Advertorial coverage
Outdoor	2:1	Paid advertising
		Bonus advertising

Is there any downside to media promotions?

Sometimes there can be a downside to media promotions. If you work with, say, one radio station, it will provide much greater value for your investment if you agree not to work with any other radio stations. But this could severely limit the amount of people in your target market that you can reach. In that case, you have two choices:

1. Offer paid and promotional exclusivity to the one radio station and get maximum value from it. Use other types of media to increase your reach.

2. Offer promotional exclusivity but not sales exclusivity, explaining that in order to achieve your objectives you need greater numbers than it can deliver alone. You will probably get less value from it as a result.

The nine steps of promotional media

Buying promotional media is very much the same as any other kind of marketing transaction. It is part science, part street smart, part creative and a lot of commonsense. Here are nine easy steps to make the task easier.

1 Set your objectives for media

Establish your specific goals. What are you trying to do? Are you promoting an event, selling tickets or building up your profile? Know what you want to accomplish, who you want to communicate with and how much you have to spend before you begin the media buying process.

2 Target your media correctly

As with above-the-line media, the key to success is to choose the media partner(s) who will deliver the largest portion of your target market for the least amount of money. For instance, the number one radio station may deliver you 115 000 listeners in your target market but you will pay to reach their total audience, which may be many times your core market.

On the other hand, if you select a lower rating radio station, magazine or television program where *their* core market is *your* core market, the likelihood is that:

➤ you will spend less money to reach more of your core audience with less media coverage waste

➤ their listeners/readers/viewers will be more receptive to your marketing message.

3 Understand why media run promotions

Competition within the media for the attention of consumers is increasing exponentially and the fact is that most media are virtually interchangeable, in terms of content.

In addition to making a sale to you, most media groups want one or more of the following things from a media promotional opportunity:

➤ To create a point of difference from their competition through the creative use of promotions. This will attract more listeners/viewers/readers and make them more attractive for regular advertisers. Creative is the key word here—if it looks or sounds like every other enter-to-win promotion in the marketplace, it isn't worth anything in a media negotiation.

➤ To increase the profile of their shows, personalities, stars, etc.

➤ To create new advertising vehicles. An example would be a newspaper creating the official program for your event in exchange for the right to sell advertising in it.

4 Create a proposal that helps them to achieve that goal

In order to maximise the media value you achieve for your investment, it is imperative that you go to your target media with a plan that will achieve your objectives and will create a strong point of difference for them and assist them with attracting their audience. Do not fall into the trap of thinking that your promotional spend is their driving force, because it is not.

5 The more creative the better

Think outside the square, push the envelope, think laterally—whatever you call it, it is about thinking creatively.

Make your proposal relevant to the audience—really think about what this audience is interested in and what they want, and then give them that and more.

Ensure your proposal really is creative. Sure, everyone wants a vacation but open up any magazine and you can enter five different contests to win a holiday at a beach resort and, with discount travel packages in every newspaper, most people know that it is not that great a deal. Be sure that what you offer is special—go to the extra effort to make this something that they could not do without you.

6 Involve your advertising agency

This is really your call but we strongly suggest that you utilise the creative resources of your advertising agency to ensure that what you propose to your target media is fully developed and creatively executed.

7 Negotiate for control of scheduling

Negotiate for time slots in programs that consistently deliver ratings and demographics you are seeking. Bargain for newspaper and magazine placements in sections that have proven circulation and the readership demographics you need.

Many media sponsorships provide advertising time at the discretion of the station. This is of absolutely no value to you. If you can't match the demographics of your audience with programs and publications that deliver to these groups, the sponsorship is of little value to you or other sponsors.

8 Never pay more than your volume rate

There are some media groups that will tell you that, since they are giving away a lot of unpaid promotion, the buy must be made at casual or 'rack' rates, even if you are a regular advertiser who normally gets a discount. This is a lot of rubbish.

If you structure your promotional offer correctly, you are actually doing them a favour—you are helping them to create a strong point of difference and paying their costs to do it. You should never pay more than the rate negotiated by you or your media buyer for the paid portion of the deal.

9 Keep your ear to the ground

Make time to meet and network with people in the media industry. These people are approachable. Learn the lingo, read industry publications and speak to your contacts to find out about the media buying process. If there is a media campaign that you feel has been particularly successful or innovative, contact the organisation and arrange to discuss the campaign with the relevant people.

Keep your ear to the ground on how radio, television and newspapers are performing. Listen to the radio and keep an eye out for industry trends, new programs and industry developments. Become an active media watcher.

A **Media Planning Worksheet** is provided below to assist you with the planning and evaluation of your media campaign.

| Media planning worksheet

Market2.doc

This worksheet is designed to assist you with the planning and evaluation of your media campaign. The items in this worksheet should be confirmed if at all possible prior to developing your sponsorship proposal. The evaluation of each type of media should be highlighted in your sponsorship proposal.

Media lingo

Negotiating media is full of a lot of lingo but, generally, you will only need to know three media words in order to discuss your media options: reach, frequency and TARPS.

Reach

Reach refers to the proportion of your target market that has the opportunity to see or hear any advertisement or advertising campaign. It is expressed as a percentage of the total market or your defined target market.

Frequency

Frequency refers to the average number of times each member of your target audience receives an advertising message over the course of the campaign.

TARPS

TARPS (Target Audience Rating Point) refers to the percentage of the target market reached over the course of an advertising campaign. It is a gross measure, taking into account both reach (the number of people that your message reaches) and frequency. For example, if there are fifteen million people in your target audience of males aged 18–34, and you achieve two hundred and fifty TARPS with your campaign, then fifteen million by 250 per cent equals 37 500 000 times that males aged 18–34 heard or saw your message. *(Cont.)*

Total media budget

	COST	VALUE
Television		
Radio		
Newspaper		
Magazines		
Outdoor		
Total		

Breakdown by media type

Television

Campaign to commence $X/X/9X$ and conclude $X/X/9X$.

Total cost: $\$X$

Total value: $\$X$

Value-to-cost ratio: X:1 (target between 3:1 to 8:1)

	DATES	NUMBER
Paid spots		
Bonus spots ('freebies')		
Promotional spots		
Production		
News coverage		
Celebrity/on-air personality appearances		

Radio

Campaign to commence $X/X/9X$ and conclude $X/X/9X$.

Total cost: $\$X$

Total value: $\$X$

Value-to-cost ratio: X:1 (target between 3:1 to 10:1)

	DATES	NUMBER
Paid spots		
Bonus spots ('freebies')		
Pre-recorded promotional spots		
Live liners (short, live promotions)		
On-air interviews		
Remote broadcast		
Celebrity/on-air personality appearances		

Media lingo *(Cont.)*

There are other media terms but these are the key ones. Even so, if you do get stuck on some terminology, just ask your media contact to explain it to you. Oftentimes, they are so immersed in the terminology that they forget that not everyone knows it.

Newspaper

Campaign to commence $X/X/9X$ and conclude $X/X/9X$.

Total cost: $\$X$

Total value: $\$X$

Value-to-cost ratio: X:1 (target between 3:1 to 8:1)

	DATES	SIZE
Paid advertising		
Bonus advertising (confirmed)		
Bonus advertising (space available)		
Program insertion (you supply the program)		
Special supplement (can be used as program)		
Advertorial coverage		

Magazine

Campaign to commence $X/X/9X$ and conclude $X/X/9X$.

Total cost: $\$X$

Total value: $\$X$

Value-to-cost ratio: X:1 (target between 2:1 to 5:1)

	DATES	SIZE
Paid advertising		
Bonus advertising		
Advertorial supplement		
Insert		
Other		

Outdoor

Campaign to commence $X/X/9X$ and conclude $X/X/9X$.

Total cost: $\$X$

Total value: $\$X$

Value-to-cost ratio: X:1 (target 2:1)

	DATES	LOCATION
24-sheets (regular sized billboards)		
Supersites (giant billboards)		
Taxis		
Buses: inside		
Buses: outside		

Publicity

Publicity includes editorial media coverage in newspaper and magazine articles, and television and radio coverage. It is also known as public relations. Public relations will probably be very important to your event. Listed below are some key strategies that you can follow that will help you gain better results from your activities.

➤ Be sure that your public relations program is handled by a reputable public relations professional, preferably a member of your national public relations institute. Hiring an independent public relations professional is probably a lot less expensive than you think. Do not dismiss spending this money until you have analysed the value against the cost.

➤ If you are handling public relations internally, do ensure that whoever handles it is an active member of the public relations community.

➤ Whether internal or external, be sure your publicist understands what is expected, the resources available to him or her, and how success will be judged. A **Publicity Brief Template** can be found below.

➤ Understand that all media is not equal. One spread in a national magazine could be worth dozens of smaller placements.

➤ Understand that, in order to get coverage, an event has to be newsworthy. Spend some time developing a variety of interesting angles. This will not only increase your potential for coverage, but it will also allow you to go to the same media outlets again and again with different stories.

➤ Do not discount the value of smaller, more targeted media outlets. They may be more receptive to your story and the readers may be more avid.

> Whether your publicity is handled internally or externally, be sure to brief them fully in writing.

Publicity brief template

Market3.doc

This is the type of document you should use when briefing a publicist (internal or external). It can also be very useful as a tender document for competitive pitching. The specifics shown here, such as media emphasis, are only to be taken as an example. This document will need to be customised to meet your needs.

Desired result

1. Strong media relations campaign supporting the launch of [*your event*].
   (a) Coverage across all media, with emphases in the following areas:
      (i) general interest
      (ii) family interest
      (iii) children/teenagers.
   (b) Close contact with targeted media to ensure the best possible coverage and story angles.
2. Increased awareness of [*your sponsors'*] sponsorship of [*your event*].
3. 100 000 attendees at [*your event*].
4. Hospitality opportunity for key customers and selected staff.

Guidelines

1. Your responsibilities for the media launch are:
    (a) Creating, mounting and tracking a top-quality publicity campaign across all media.
    (b) Working with [*your event*] to create an effective media kit.
    (c) All creative and administrative aspects of the media launch to the following rough guidelines:

    Timing: to be determined

    Location: to be determined

    Theme: to be determined

    Featuring: celebrities, demonstrations, etc.

    (d) Development of a guest list and invitations (in conjunction with the above). Invitees will include:
       (i)   the media
       (ii)   celebrities
       (iii) sponsors
       (iv)   representatives of [*your event*]
       (v)   Parliamentary Minister of *X*
       (vi)   sponsor's costumed character.
    (e) Co-ordinating photographic opportunities, interviews and other special requests as they pertain to publicity.
    (f) Full and accurate accounting of expenses and fees.

2. Timetable
    (a) Preliminary publicity plan to [*your event*] by [*date*].
    (b) [*Your event*] to open lines of communication between publicist and sponsors/celebrities when publicity plan is approved.
    (c) Publicist to enact publicity plan and begin campaign (to magazines, television and other alternative media that need longer lead times) by [*date*].
    (d) The launch is planned for [*date*]. Time of day to be determined but suggest late morning.

3. Communications
    (a) We will expect weekly updates on publicity progress, including a list of placements, confirmation that placements have been clipped and compiled, and responses to invitations.
    (b) We will include publicist on all pertinent communications.
    (c) Specific requests for information, both ways, should be put in writing.

[*Your event*] Resources

1. Information available:
    (a) background information on the *X*-year history of the event
    (b) examples of media coverage in past years
    (c) biographies of celebrities
    (d) overall marketing plan
    (e) implementation timeline
    (f) budget.

2. Information to be confirmed:
    (a) celebrities available for launch
    (b) sponsors/staff to be invited.

3. Materials currently available:
    (a) creative look developed by [*designer or advertising agency*]
    (b) completed advertisements
    (c) bromides of event and sponsor logos
    (d) photographs of celebrities and VIP guests
    (e) biographical sheets for all celebrities
    (f) a range of banners and flags
    (g) T-shirts and caps.

4. Materials in development:
    (a) creative piece for media launch invitation
    (b) sponsor utilisation of sponsorship (main media support).

5. The team
    Although there are many other people involved in this event, the team includes
    the key contacts.
    (a) Jane Chen, Marketing Manager for [*your event*]. Overall responsibility for the
         project. Phone (852) 2555 5555, fax (852) 2555 5551.
    (b) Larry Lunar, Marketing Co-ordinator of [*your event*]. Providing assistance in the
         planning, co-ordination and implementation of the sponsorship and supporting
         marketing activities. Phone (852) 2555 5554, fax (852) 2555 5551.

6. Celebrities available
    List celebrities, athletes or other well-known participants.

7. Budget
    There will be an absolute ceiling of $*X* for all costs associated with this publicity
    campaign, which cannot be overrun.

8. Evaluation to be based on:

   (a) weight of the campaign and balance of media gained

   (b) impact and innovative style of media launch

   (c) management process and communication.

Source

[Your name]

[Your event]

[Full address]

[Phone, fax, e-mail]

Database marketing

One of the best ways to communicate large amounts of information to a specific target market is to embark upon a campaign of database marketing.

Databases come in all shapes and size and you probably have access to several. Below we have listed several sources, in order of their probable receptiveness to your marketing message:

1. members

2. season ticket holders

3. previous attendees or ticket purchasers

4. people who have signed up for your mailing list

5. databases provided by industry organisations (e.g. your local arts governing body)

6. databases that you rent from outside sources (demographically and geographically targeted).

Once you have settled on the database(s) to be used for your communications, you will need to determine how you will reach this group. Keep in mind that different types of databases represent different groups that may be receptive to varying methods of communication. You have many options for communication, including:

➤ newsletters or other publications

➤ putting information in regular mailings

➤ special mailings (specific to this event)

➤ telemarketing

➤ broadcast fax

➤ promotional material in member gathering places (clubhouse, etc.)

You probably have more access to databases than you realise.

➤ Internet sites

➤ e-mail (ensure each recipient has authorised you to broadcast e-mail information to them).

In addition to informing them about your event or organisation, you may also want to include some type of enticement for them to attend. Some suggestions include:

➤ priority seating

➤ early ticketing

➤ special pricing or offers

➤ merchandise discounts

➤ invitations to special events.

Signage

Signage includes signs that are made specifically for an event, such as banners, A-frames and scoreboards. Pre-event and event signage can be a strong communication vehicle. Think broadly about your options, which could include:

➤ venue signage (facing a roadway or public area)

➤ signage on your office building (if it is in a good location)

➤ street banners or flags around your town

➤ electronic billboards (many cities and towns have electronic reader-boards that show upcoming events)

➤ signage at convention and visitor bureau kiosks

> Any surface that can be painted, bannered or hung from can support signage.

VEHICLE SIGNAGE

> perimeter signage
> airport signage
> vehicle signage.

The Internet

With an ever-increasing proportion of the marketplace getting onto the information superhighway, you cannot neglect this powerful communications medium.

If at all possible, you should set up your own Web site, outlining key information, such as:

> what the event or organisation is
> location
> dates and times
> pricing
> parking
> schedule of events
> special offers
> other points of interest
> logos of all sponsors (linked to their sites)
> logos of all endorsing bodies (linked to their sites).

If you don't have a Web site, you should still try to get this information onto the Internet—listing it on as many as possible of the following sites:

> convention and visitor bureau schedule of events
> city council schedule of events

➤ governing body schedule of events (e.g. if it is a golf event, ensure that your state and national endorsing golf bodies list your event on their calendar)

➤ newspaper 'What's On' sites (some radio and television stations have this type of listing on their sites, too)

➤ your sponsor's sites

➤ sites specific to your target market (e.g. teenagers, football fans, retirees, etc.).

In any case, ensure that your Web site is listed under a wide variety of key words with all of the major Internet search engines.

If you don't have a Web site, you should still try to get your event onto the Net through other sites.

Part 2

sales

The sales process

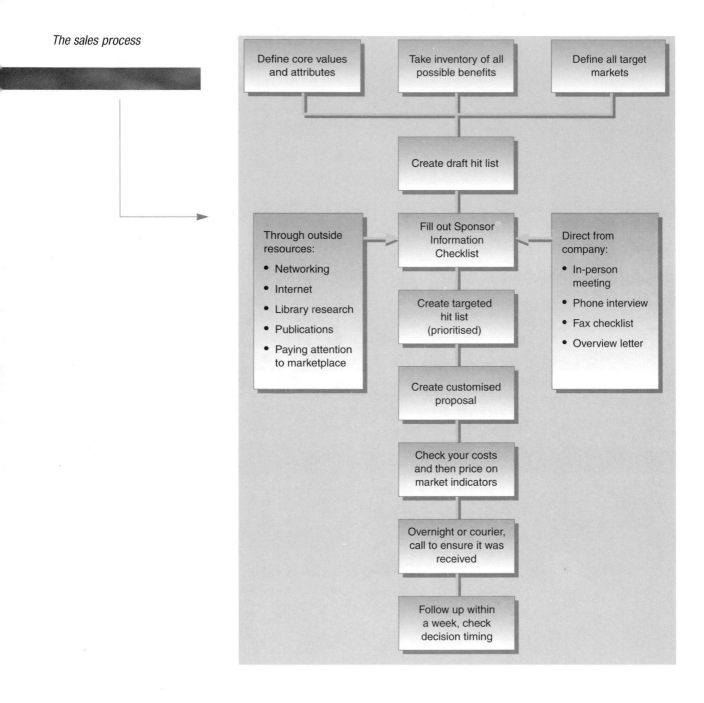

Chapter 4

Understand what you have to offer

When most sponsorship seekers, particularly non-sporting organisations, are asked to define what they have to offer, they either start listing all of the places where they can place a sponsor's logo or they talk at great length about all of the good corporate citizenship a company will foster by supporting them. Either way, it's the wrong answer.

In general terms, a sponsor wants three things from a sponsee:

1. To be associated with the core values and attributes of a sponsee, with the goal being to introduce or reinforce those attributes within its company or product— this process is called image transfer.

2. To access one or more of the target markets of a sponsee and to reach these people with the sponsor's marketing message in a meaningful way.

3. To gain a range of tangible benefits from the sponsee, ensuring that the impact of the previous two points is maximised and providing mechanisms and tools to achieve specific marketing objectives.

If you want to maximise your chances of creating a strong match with a sponsor, it is imperative that you understand fully what you offer in each of these areas and thus, the more precisely you can define these benefits, the better.

Define your core values and attributes

While defining core values and attributes may sound like a difficult and tedious process, it's really not that difficult if you get yourself into the right frame of mind and then approach it step by step.

First, rather than putting a lot of pressure on yourself, try to imagine this as a very straightforward process of describing the personality of your event or organisation. It's that simple. In fact, if you find yourself struggling with this process, try practising all of the steps below using your best friend or spouse as the subject first, and then move on to your event.

Figure 4.1 Identified attributes and core values of the play Beautiful Thing

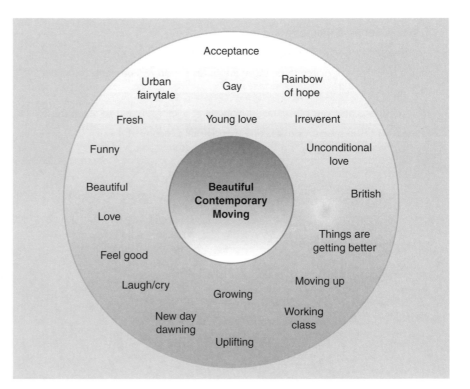

1. On a whiteboard or big piece of paper, draw a big circle with a smaller circle in the centre of it.

2. In the outside circle, write down every word you can think of that describes the personality of your event (e.g. fun, celebration, youthful, New York tradition, etc.). Think broadly. Involve your team and spend 15–30 minutes brainstorming. What you come up with are the attributes of your event.

3. Once you are satisfied that you have characterised the personality of your event, you need to distil this definition into two or three words that truly encompass what your event is about, what it stands for to your target audience and how it makes them feel. One or more of these words may already appear among your attributes but don't worry, that's normal.

As an example, Figure 4.1 shows the attributes and core values identified by a small professional theatre company, Make Believe Productions, for the Australian tour of Jonathan Harvey's play, *Beautiful Thing*.

Define your audience

You have already defined your target markets when you developed your marketing plan. Now, you need to re-look at your target markets from the sponsor's perspective.

Your marketing objective is to get people to your event. This is quite different from the sponsor's marketing objective, which is to communicate its marketing message to as much of its target market as possible. Thus, when defining your target market in terms of what you can offer a sponsor, you need to look at the audience in terms of the people who will be receiving your (and, subsequently, your sponsor's) marketing message.

When you look at target audiences in terms of what you have to offer a sponsor, be absolutely certain that you don't fixate on the people who actually come to your event. No matter how many people attend, or how well suited they are to your potential sponsor, they still reflect only a fraction of the sponsor's target marketplace.

Through your marketing efforts, you will reach a lot of people who will not attend your event for one reason or another but who are still receptive to the marketing message. These people could include people who see or hear:

➤ pre-event advertising

➤ pre-event promotions (direct marketing, Internet sites, sponsor promotions, etc.)

➤ pre-event publicity

➤ street, venue or event signage

> When communicating with a sponsor, define your audience in terms of everyone who will receive your marketing message, not just the people who will attend.

➤ media coverage of the event

➤ post-event wrap-up coverage.

Take inventory

In order to understand the full range of tangible benefits your organisation has to offer, you need to prepare an inventory of your assets. Make a list of every promotional and marketing opportunity that could possibly be of value to a potential sponsor. List everything, even if you wouldn't sell it. This helps you to think expansively and you can sort them out later.

During this process, you need to look at your organisation as a sponsor would. You will no doubt be astounded at the wide range of benefits that you have to offer that you have never thought of before. This should allow you to showcase the value of your organisation to a much broader range of sponsors.

Once you have prepared this list, do not make the mistake of offering your entire inventory to sponsors (we have seen this done before). Instead, think of your inventory as your kitchen. It is a list of everything you have in your kitchen that could be used to make a meal—the food, the spices, the utensils, appliances and even the electricity in the wall. Imagine what a mess you would get in if you tried to make a meal using everything in your kitchen. That's the same kind of mess you will get in if you try to create an offer using every item on your inventory. What you need is a recipe and we'll provide you with one.

A **Generic Inventory** can be found below to get you started. Just keep adding to and subtracting from it until it reflects what your organisation has to offer and, remember, this is a living document—update it regularly.

Never offer a sponsor everything on your inventory.

Generic inventory

Sales1.doc

What follows is a generic inventory. This is a starting point for you to prepare an inventory of your own property. The point of this exercise is to ensure you catalogue everything that you control which could be of value to a potential sponsor. You will probably not use all or even most of these items but it creates a menu from which to develop customised proposals for your potential sponsors.

Sponsorship types

➤ Naming rights sponsorship (perceived 'ownership' of the event)

➤ Presenting sponsorship

➤ Naming rights or presenting sponsorship of a section, area, entry or team

➤ Naming rights or presenting sponsorship of a day, weekend or week at the event

➤ Naming rights or presenting sponsorship of an event-driven award, trophy or scholarship

➤ Naming rights or presenting sponsorship of a related or subordinated event

➤ Supporting sponsorship

➤ Official product

➤ Preferred supplier

Exclusivity

➤ Category exclusivity among sponsors at or below a given level

➤ Category exclusivity among sponsors at any level

➤ Category exclusivity in event-driven advertising or promotional media

➤ Category exclusivity as a supplier or seller at the event

Licence and endorsements

➤ Use of logo(s) and trademark(s) for media and sales promotions and supporting materials

➤ Merchandising rights

➤ Product endorsement (personal or organisation)

Contracts

➤ Discounts for multi-year contracts

➤ First right of refusal for new sponsorship at conclusion of contract

➤ Performance incentives

Vesting

➤ A portion of the overall net profits

➤ A portion of the proceeds from a part of the event (ticket sales, concessions, parking, exhibitors, etc.)

Venue

➤ Input in venue, route and/or timing

➤ Use of sponsor venue for launch, main event or supporting event

Media profile

➤ Inclusion in all print, outdoor and/or broadcast advertising (logo or name)

➤ Inclusion on event promotional pieces (posters, fliers, brochures, buttons, apparel, etc.—logo or name)

➤ Advertising time during a televised event

➤ Event-driven promotional radio or television schedule

➤ Event-driven outdoor advertising (billboards, vehicle, public transport)

➤ Sponsor/retailer share media (theme display advertising, 30/30 or 15/15 broadcast)

➤ Advertising space in event program, catalogue and so on

Media production

➤ Broadcast rights (exclusive or non-exclusive)

➤ Production of event-driven broadcast or print advertising

➤ Production of event-driven videos for promotion, training or documentation

On-site

➤ Sampling opportunities

➤ Demonstration/display opportunities

➤ Opportunities to sell products on-site (exclusive or non-exclusive)

➤ Distribution of coupons, information or premiums

Signage

➤ Venue signage (full, partial or non-broadcast view)

➤ Inclusion in on-site event signage (exclusive or non-exclusive)

➤ Inclusion on pre-event street banners, flags and so on

➤ Press conference signage

➤ Vehicle signage

➤ Event participant uniforms/pinnies/number tags

➤ Event staff shirts/caps/uniforms

Hospitality arrangements

➤ Tickets to the event (luxury boxes, preferred seating, reserved seating or general admission)

➤ VIP tickets/passes (backstage, sideline, pit passes, press box, etc.)

➤ Celebrity—participant meet and greets

➤ Event-related travel arrangements, administration and chaperones (consumer prizes, VIP or trade incentives)

Public relations

➤ Inclusion in all press releases and other media activities

➤ Inclusion in sponsor-related and media activities

➤ Public relations campaigns designed for sponsor's market (consumer or trade)

Production

➤ Event design and production

➤ Producing a special event specifically for the sponsor

➤ Other design and production (uniform, props, set, stage, costumes, etc.)

➤ Hiring and/or administration of temporary or contract personnel, services and vendors

➤ Logistical assistance, including technical or creative expertise

Cause tie-in

➤ An opportunity to involve the sponsor's preferred charitable organisation or cause

➤ Donation of a percentage of ticket or product sales to a charity

Ancillary or supporting events

➤ Tickets or invitations available to ancillary parties, receptions, shows, launches and so on

➤ Signage, sampling and other benefits available around ancillary parties, receptions, shows and launches

Research and evaluation

➤ Access to pre- and/or post-event research (quantitative or qualitative, attendees or general public)

➤ Opportunity to provide sponsorship or industry-oriented questions on post-event research

➤ Post-event value-to-cost analysis

➤ Full event and sponsorship documentation (as above plus newspaper/magazine clippings, broadcast coverage, photos, etc.)

Retail sell-on

➤ Right of a retailer sponsor to on-sell sponsorship benefits to vendors in specific product categories

Contra

➤ Opportunity to provide equipment, services, technology, expertise or personnel useful to the success of the event in trade for part of a sponsorship fee

➤ Opportunity to provide media value, in-store/in-house promotion in trade for part of a sponsorship fee

➤ Opportunity to provide media at sponsor-contracted discounted rates in trade for part of a sponsorship fee

Information technology

➤ Signage or banners about the event on Internet sites

➤ Promotion or contests on the event on Internet sites

➤ Links to the sponsor Internet site from the event Internet site

➤ Naming rights (perceived 'ownership') to the event Internet site

➤ Banners or promotion on the event CD-ROM

➤ Licence to produce an event-oriented CD-ROM for promotion or sale

Other promotional opportunities

➤ Custom-design and administration of media promotions

➤ Custom-design and administration of sales promotions (consumer and trade)

➤ Sell-in to trade of sales promotions

➤ Design, production and distribution of point-of-sale material

➤ Design of on-pack promotion and liaison with factory (packaging and distribution)

➤ Securing and administration of entertainment, celebrity appearances and so on

➤ Provision by the sponsor of spokesperson/people, celebrity appearances, costumed character and so on to enhance association

➤ Proofs of purchase for discount admission

➤ Proofs of purchase for discount or free parking

➤ Proofs of purchase for premium item (on site)

➤ Proof of mail-in or telephone-in redemption

➤ Opportunity to provide prizes for media or event promotions

➤ Coupons/advertising on backs of tickets

➤ Discount admission coupons for customers (distributed in-pack or POP)

Database/relationship marketing

➤ Unlimited access to event-generated database(s) for direct marketing follow-up

➤ Opportunity to provide inserts in event-oriented mailings

➤ Rental of event database for one-off communications

➤ Opportunity to run database-generating raffles or contests on site as a requirement for attendee admission

Consulting

➤ Evaluation and recommendations regarding participation in new and existing opportunities

➤ Pre-event research (market, site, demographic, psychographic, feasibility, budgeting)

➤ Assistance in determining objectives and basis for quantifying results

Chapter 5

Creating a hit list

Once you understand your target markets and what you have to offer, you should start developing a preliminary hit list of potential sponsors. In fact, you will often start thinking of companies when you go through the previous exercises.

When creating a list of potential sponsors, be sure to pay attention to *specific products* or *services*, not just the overall corporation. We cannot emphasise this enough. There are three reasons for this.

1. Very few companies offer only one product and, where there are multiple products, they are often very different from each other. Their differing attributes and target markets will fit with varying types of sponsorships.

2. Corporate sponsorship departments are usually the first place that sponsees go with their proposals and hence they are inundated with requests. Going directly to a well-matched brand area can minimise the competition you will face for both attention and money. (Please note, this does not always work but it is worth a try.)

3. The brand areas will often have their own marketing budgets. These areas are most closely accountable for the performance of their brands and are often willing

to put marketing funds that are not specifically ear-marked for sponsorship into this type of investment if they believe they will get a positive result.

Sponsor matching

A good hit list will be based upon matching your event or property with a sponsor. There are three ways of doing this:

➤ by target markets

➤ by objectives

➤ by attributes/values.

The power is where two or more of these matches intersect.

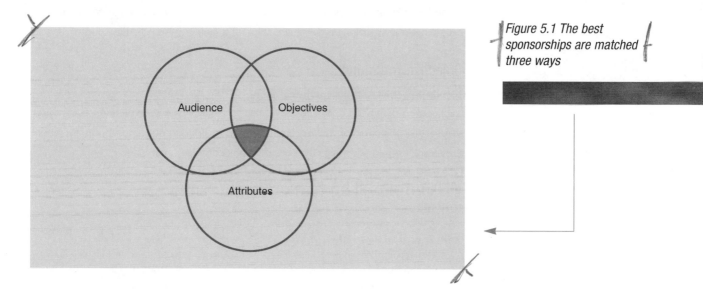

> When looking at potential sponsors, look at specific products or services, not just the corporation.

Figure 5.1 The best sponsorships are matched three ways

Audience matching

The starting point for sponsor matching is ensuring that your event or product targets one or more of the sponsor's core audiences. The more of your target markets that match the sponsor's target markets, the more potential there is for a strong sponsorship. If you don't match any of the potential sponsor's target markets, then it does not matter how well you match objectives or attributes, you are wasting your time.

There are several types of sponsor audiences that you could match:

➤ current customers

➤ potential customers that fit one of the sponsor's current customer profiles

➤ newly targeted potential customer groups

➤ intermediary customers (retailers, trade, distribution)

➤ internal customers (sponsor employees).

There is one common pitfall surrounding newly targeted customer groups. Often, sponsorship seekers will realise that their event does not target any of a company's different markets. Instead, they try to make a case that they can deliver new markets. Although this approach is very proactive, it rarely works.

When a company targets a new group of customers, the initiative is usually developed through market research and accompanied by a comprehensive marketing campaign. If the company has not already identified your marketplace as having a potential for them, it is unlikely that they will be receptive to your approach, particularly within your time frame. In addition, one sponsorship on its own is unlikely to deliver the critical mass of people needed to make the new marketplace desirable for the potential sponsor.

Objective matching

This type of matching does not always happen but it can be a very powerful tool for gaining sponsorship if it does. Objective matching happens when you and your sponsor share actual objectives, such as 'promoting good health and nutrition to primary school students', or when your objectives are mutually complementary.

Example: The bank and the show

An established overseas ice show is touring New Zealand for the first time. It has a substantial media budget to promote ticket sales but its experience elsewhere has been that, the more different ways it can speak to its target market of families with children aged 2–10, the better result it gets.

A major New Zealand bank with branches throughout the country is facing increased competition from new entrants into the home loan market. It is particularly feeling the pinch with younger, first-time home buyers who are being attracted by the lower interest rates offered by the new competition. It is also losing current customers, who are switching away to the competition's lower rates. The Bank has

countered this by creating a range of innovative home finance products. It is looking for ways to entice current and new customers to look into the new products and understand how they work, as well as to add value to its relationship with existing customers.

The Show and the Bank were able to achieve objectives for each other in a number of ways:

• The Bank created displays in every branch across New Zealand, including monitors playing a promotional video of the Show for people waiting in line. This ran for a month prior and through the tour.

• The Bank promoted the Show on all ATM machine screens for the same time period.

- The Bank included fliers for the Show in customer statements, offering priority ticketing as an added value for all customers.
- The Bank promoted to current and potential customers that they would get one free child's ticket for every adult ticket purchased if they filled in a questionnaire and ran a computer model of how their home loan would work using the new home loan product. This could take place either in the branch or on the Internet.
- The Show provided a list of all ticket buyers to the Bank after the tour. The Bank knows that families with young children are prime candidates for home loans and used this list for database marketing.

Attribute matching

Strong attribute matching is one of the hallmarks of great sponsorship. It creates relevance between the sponsor and your event, which carries through, creating relevance and interest in the sponsorship to your target markets.

Look at the list of attributes and values of your event that you prepared in Chapter 4. Just as there are different levels to your organisation's personality, there are also different levels in how you can match with a potential sponsor.

➤ Your values, in the centre circle, are the core of what you are about. Matching one or more of these with a sponsor is absolutely essential in order to foster the image transfer that most sponsors are trying to achieve.

➤ Attributes, in the outer circle, are the areas where you can define yourself to best match a potential sponsor. This is where you can be somewhat of a chameleon, creating a strong and relevant appeal to a wide range of potential sponsors.

When identifying potential attribute matches, remember that there are two different ways of matching:

1. **Attribute equals attribute.** For example, a women's contemporary art exhibition has the attributes of being smart, strong, sexy and original. This may be a good match with Calvin Klein fragrances, who market themselves in the same way.

2. **Sponsor attribute solves sponsee attribute.** For example, being a member of a rally driving team has to be one of the world's dirtiest occupations. This may be a good match for a laundry soap, car wash, personal care products or Black and Decker's Dustbuster.

Promoting a strong attribute match can be a big selling point. When used in an interesting or humorous way, attribute matching can lead to new approaches to creative advertising and is a great way for a company to cut through the clutter of a heavily sponsored event.

Case study: The International Chili Society and Procter and Gamble

The International Chili Society holds cook-offs around the world, culminating annually in the World's Championship Chili Cook-off, an enormous festival of hot food enjoyed by tens of thousands of people.

One of our all-time favourite sponsorships featured a company that was not a huge sponsor of this event but the attribute-driven shock value provided an impact that far outstripped many of the other, larger sponsors.

Just imagine some of the attributes of chilli. Delicious as it may be, there are some rather specific traits that can be often be attributed to eating the stuff, some of them problematic—heartburn and indigestion.

So, who was that sponsor that everyone remembered? Procter and Gamble's Pepto Bismol Antacid.

Matching three ways

Case study: American Express and the Museum of Contemporary Art

The Museum of Contemporary Art is one of Australia's pre-eminent cultural organisations. It was seeking an interesting way of displaying part of its extensive permanent collection and developed the concept 'Plastic Fantastic' around a planned exhibition of the use of plastic from the 1960s through to the current day.

At the same time, American Express was preparing to introduce a new Blue Card, aimed primarily at a young, up and coming audience.

This 1997 sponsorship is an outstanding example of a sponsor and sponsee who are matched in all three ways.

Target market matching

American Express was trying to reach younger, sophisticated professionals living in the Sydney metropolitan area—not the core marketplace for their other cards. This matched extremely well with the Museum's audience:

- 45 per cent were 25–34 years old
- 50 per cent were earning over $50 000 annually
- 63 per cent were single
- 53 per cent were professional
- 74 per cent resided in inner suburbs
- 60 per cent socialised in cafes and bars.

This is a good example of a sponsee delivering a new target market to a sponsor.

Attribute matching

The Blue Card was being launced with the taglines 'young, funky and individual' and 'life's there, go out and grab it'. These attributes are virtually a perfect match with the well-known attributes of the Museum of Contemporary Art.

Matching a charge card or 'plastic' and an exhibition of plastic items is also strong.

The match was further extended with the commission of a large, blue plastic sculpture, the 'Blue Boy', which was displayed prominently outside the Museum in its prime city location throughout the exhibition.

Objective matching

One of American Express' key objectives was to create added value for its cardholders. Two of the Museum of Contemporary Art's objectives were to sample the exhibition to opinion leaders in their target demographic market and to sell more merchandise in their store.

The two organisations worked together to achieve these objectives by offering American Express members special discounts in the Museum store, as well as by creating cardholder days at the Museum, when members got free entry.

Research your potential sponsors

If you ask a sponsor, any sponsor, what they want from a sponsorship proposal, they will invariably say one thing: 'We want a proposal that is tailored to our needs'. The big question is how do you know what they need?

Now that you know how you can match with a potential sponsor, you need to get the information that will allow you to assess their suitability—do you match?—as well as allowing you to create an offer that meets their needs.

Your *job* as a sponsee is to assist your sponsor in meeting their needs. In order to do that, you should know your potential sponsor's:

- long-term marketing objectives (over twelve months)
- short-term marketing objectives
- product or brand attributes
- target markets
- needs—absolute requirements
- wants—these are things that would be nice
- exclusions—many companies, for instance, will not sponsor individuals, and some

Do not develop
your offer until
you have
completed the
Sponsor
Information
Checklist for your
potential sponsor.

will not be involved if an alcohol company is a prime sponsor, so you need to
know these things

➤ special emphases—basically everything else, such as new product launches, new
services being offered, a new logo, their competitive situation, etc.

In Chapter 4 when we discussed creating an inventory of your assets we compared
the inventory to a kitchen. Well, the research you gather about your potential sponsor
is your recipe.

A **Sponsor Information Checklist** can be found on page 83 and this will
help you to compile and organise this information. Completing this checklist will
provide you with a strong understanding of what a potential sponsor requires from
a sponsorship investment. It should be completed in full prior to developing your
offer.

As you complete the checklist for each of the companies on your preliminary hit
list, you will notice that a number of potential sponsors will emerge as being very
strongly matched with your event, some less so, and many companies will be excluded
altogether. This process will save you a lot of time, as you will then only approach the
most likely sponsors. It will also demonstrate to potential sponsors that your primary
aim in sponsorship is to understand what they need to achieve and to help them
achieve it.

The ways of obtaining the information for the **Sponsor Information Checklist**
are listed in the table on page 81.

FROM THE SPONSOR	FROM OTHER SOURCES
Sponsorship guidelines	Networking
In-person meetings	Internet
Telephone interview	Library
Fax request for information	Publications
Annual report	Paying attention to the marketplace

Outlined below are these sources in the order in which they should be utilised or approached.

Other sources

Before you even bother picking up the telephone to call a company, you need to research them thoroughly through other sources. If you have a list of prospects, a couple of afternoons spent on the Internet and at the library can provide you with a lot of information.

Use this information to fill out, as completely as possible, the **Sponsor Information Checklist** for each of your potential sponsors.

A range of research, news and networking resources is included in the Appendix.

Annual report

If your potential sponsor is a publicly listed company, their annual report must be made available to anyone that asks. The usefulness of information in annual reports varies but can include some or all of the following:

➤ an understanding of the corporate culture, mission and vision

➤ a list of all products and brand lines

➤ the overall financial performance of the company (and often specific product categories, as well)

➤ annual expenditure on sponsorship

➤ a list of all (or sometimes only major) sponsorships

➤ new company initiatives

➤ income and expenditure trends.

You should review the annual reports of any potential sponsors prior to creating an offer but do remember that this is only a starting place. You need to know much more specific information to create an effective proposal.

Annual reports may be requested from the public affairs area of the company's headquarters. Do not request it from the marketing or sponsorship areas—you will look silly.

> Request annual reports from the public affairs area, not marketing.

Use the Internet
to research
overseas corporate
headquarters of
your potential
sponsors.

With the advent of the Internet, many companies are also making their annual reports available on the Web. This is not only convenient but can be a great resource when you are researching a multinational company with an overseas head office, as it allows you to get not only a national but also a global understanding of their culture, direction and priorities.

Sponsorship guidelines

The fastest, cleanest and usually most complete way to get the required information from a sponsor is to request a copy of their **Sponsorship Guidelines**. This is (usually) a short document that outlines all of their needs, exclusions, target markets and the process by which they make investment decisions.

This can be a fantastic resource for you but beware of preprinted, glossy brochures. Sponsors' needs change all the time and they can sometimes be out of date. We advise sponsors to put their guidelines on letterhead and update them regularly. This method may be less slick but the information is often more reliable.

Although **Sponsorship Guidelines** are gaining popularity with sponsors, not all companies have them. If you come across one that does not, you can make yourself look great and add value to your relationship by providing our version of this valuable tool to them. Clearly, the **Sponsorship Guidelines** that we have provided are just an example that the sponsor will need to customise to reflect their unique needs and positioning. A copy of the **Sponsorship Guidelines** can be found on page 87.

In-person meetings

No matter how much information you find about a company from other sources, it is always ideal to meet with a potential sponsor prior to developing a proposal. There are several reasons for this:

➤ you will gain a lot more insight from a conversation than from even the best proposal guidelines

➤ you will develop a personal relationship with the sponsorship manager

➤ your enthusiasm and belief in the project will often be infectious

➤ it is more difficult for someone to brush you off if you are sitting there in person.

Be sure to do your homework before your in-person meeting. You should endeavour to fill out as much as possible of your **Sponsor Information Checklist** before making contact. This will allow you to demonstrate your professionalism and commitment to understanding their needs. You can also use what you know about the company and its sponsorship program to find out what has and has not worked for them in the past, how sponsorships were utilised and

Do your homework
on the company
before the
meeting.

other pertinent pieces of information. For specific meeting techniques, see the **Sales Checklist** on page 108.

Telephone interview

If you cannot have a meeting in person with the potential sponsor, a telephone interview is definitely the next best thing. Again, it is absolutely imperative to do your homework prior to picking up the telephone or you could do more harm than good.

Do make an appointment for the interview, just as if you were there in person, and stick to your allotted time.

Fax request for information

If you don't have any joy contacting the sponsor directly, you could send a fax request for information. You can either use the fax to request a short, information-gathering meeting or telephone call, or you can request specific information from them in order to complete your sponsor information checklist.

If you choose to use the latter approach, we suggest that you use your word processor to create a very short form, complete with check boxes and the like. Ask only for the information you have not been able to get through outside research, as well as any specific questions you may have. Generally, the simpler you make the request, the more likely it is that the contact will respond, so you should endeavour to create a fax form that can be filled out in no more than 2–3 minutes.

Sponsor information checklist

Sales2.doc

The idea of the sponsor information checklist is to provide you with a format so that you can obtain as much information about your target sponsor as you possibly can, by giving you all of the clues you need to make your best shot at gaining their sponsorship. Do not worry if you cannot get all of the information but do try to get most of it before creating your offer.

If you speak to your potential sponsor, be reasonable about the amount of information you request and the time you need to have this information in. Know the basics and ask the questions below that are in italics first. Also, get the correct address, name and title from the receptionist or secretary, not your target contact.

Sponsor: ....

Address ....

Phone .... Fax ....

Contact name ....

Title ....

Secretary name ....

First step, request an annual report (if they are a public company).   ·   ❑ Done

Key brand/product attributes:

1. ....

2. ....

3. ....

4. ....

5. ....

Objectives:

1. ....

2. ....

3. ....

4. ....

5. ....

Relevant product lines and target markets:

PRODUCT	TARGET MARKETS

Have they recently or are they planning to add to or extend their brand lines, change their logo, re-launch a product, merge with another company or enter into a new or distinctive marketing campaign? Please describe.

....

....

....

....

....

Key direct competitors in their category.

1. ....

2. ....

3. ....

4. ....

5. ....

Key indirect competitors (other categories that may compete with their category).

1. ....

2. ....

3. ....

4. ....

5. ....

How do they utilise their sponsorships?

....

....

Has this company ever sponsored a similar property? Can you get any information on how that
went? (Speak to the other sponsee if you feel it is appropriate.)

....

....

....

....

Is there any national or overseas precedent for a relationship such as this? Have you got a copy
of any supporting magazine or newspaper articles?

....

....

Do they have any exclusions in the area of sponsorship?

....

....

How long should approval take and what is the approval procedure for sponsorships?

....

....

....

....

....

Date: ....

Information gathered by: ....

Sponsorship guidelines

Sales3.doc

[*Sponsor name*] receives dozens of proposals every year, many of which we reject because they do not adequately meet our needs. We have developed this document to make our requirements clear to potential sponsorship seekers and to encourage the presentation of proposals that meet those needs. [*Information here to be taken as examples only.*]

General

➤ We will consider proposals in all categories except [*insert any exclusions or limitations here*].

➤ We generally need a minimum of six months lead time.

➤ Logo exposure is considered a bonus but is not the primary goal of sponsorship.

➤ We prefer to invest in sponsorships that carry out audience research during and/or after the event, including sponsor questions, and provide results to the sponsor.

Core brand values/attributes

To assist you in understanding our positioning, here is an overview of our core brand values and attributes:

➤ 'What's Best about America' (tag line)

➤ an American icon product

➤ high quality

➤ relaxation

➤ manly (full-strength beers)

➤ 'Drink Responsibly' message.

Sponsorships must provide at least six of the following

These points should be tied to both your overall objectives and key attributes.

➤ A natural link with [*insert key product attributes here*]

➤ Creative ideas for utilisation of the sponsorship

➤ Exclusive vending rights

➤ Retail cross-promotion

➤ Investment divided into an upfront fee plus a performance-based incentive

➤ Naming rights

- On-site sales
- Opportunity provided for key customer hospitality ('what money cannot buy' activities are particularly good)
- Provide promotional main media time/space (logo exposure does not count)
- Specifically target one of our primary demographic groups
- Sponsorship exclusivity

To be considered proposals must include

- Key details of the opportunity
- Overview of your marketing plan—including what is and is not confirmed
- List of sponsors who have committed to date
- A comprehensive list of benefits, including how they relate to us and our product(s)
- A timeline, including important deadlines
- Credentials of your company and key subcontractors (publicist, event producer, etc.)

Process for consideration

- All proposals are reviewed by the Sponsorship Manager to assess suitability, feasibility, and resources required (human and monetary)
- Recommended proposals are presented to [*insert title*] for approval
- The sponsee is notified of the disposition of the proposal within *X* weeks

Target markets and positioning

Do not give anything secret away here, but the sponsor should name the products, their positioning and key markets. An example is provided.

Product A	Males, 18–30, sports and social scene oriented, 'manly', use high-adventure sports as key aspect of marketing
Product B	Primary: Designated drivers
	Secondary: Women 18+
Product C	Males 25+, up and coming, ABC+, quality oriented, highly brand aware
Product D	Hoteliers and upmarket restaurants, available east coast only
Product E	Males and females, 18–24, single, introducing new flavour in July 1999

Chapter 6

Proposals

We'll now go back to our kitchen analogy. You have an inventory of all of your ingredients, the sponsor information checklist has provided you with a recipe, so now it's time to start cooking!

What to include in a proposal

In order to give the sponsor enough information to make a decision, a proposal must contain the following points.

Overview

Paint the picture, tantalise the sponsor with both what your organisation is about and how you can benefit them.

Event/property details

This is really an information sheet listing dates, times, locations, projected attendance, ticket costs, membership numbers and so on—all the hard data. The information provided here could vary widely depending on the type of property.

Marketing plan

This is an overview of the marketing plan you have already created. It outlines exactly how you will be marketing yourself, the value of all marketing components, which media you are using and your publicity plan.

Market research

If you want to sell sponsorship, you really should have comprehensive market research information or at the very least a detailed profile of your marketplace—who they are, their income and education levels, where they live and so on. Do not use phrases such as 'lovers of art', 'museum-goers' or 'general audience'. These types of phrases are too general and indicate to sponsors that you know nothing about your audience.

Examples

This is where you get to strut your stuff and demonstrate your understanding of your potential sponsor's needs. Tell them how you are going to solve their problems. Tell them how you are going to achieve their goals.

Comprehensive list of benefits

This is where you list the benefits that you will provide as part of this offer. These should be taken from your inventory and reflect a comprehensive package but should never include everything in your inventory. Tailoring the list is absolutely essential.

Use bullet points and, depending upon how long the list is, you may want to categorise the benefits as they are categorised on your inventory.

Investment

This should reflect the total investment, including:

➤ cash

➤ contra or in-kind investment

➤ promotional support that directly benefits your organisation.

You should also include payment due dates and any performance incentives in this section.

Bonuses

Your case for investment will be a lot stronger if you can provide the potential sponsor with a precedent as to exactly how this has worked for other companies like them and/or a precedent as to exactly how your other sponsors have achieved a commercial return. If you have this information, put it in a section before the 'Comprehensive list of benefits'.

How long should it be?

As a rough guideline, in order to get all of the information into the proposal that the sponsor will need, you are looking at a minimum of four to five pages. If you have a lot of promotional concepts, research, precedents or a very comprehensive marketing plan, you could go up to about twelve pages. Any more than that and you risk losing your reader.

More important than size, however, is that it is easy and fast to read. This will be more a testament to your ability to format the proposal nicely and use concise wording than the actual amount of information included.

The teaser

You may want to create a two- to three-page proposal summary of the property, target audience, key marketing and promotional strategies and key benefits. We have found it very effective to use the summary to tease out prospective sponsors, which can greatly assist you, particularly if time is of the essence. Do be prepared to customise this summary wherever and whenever possible and ensure you include contact details and deadlines for decisions.

Using the sponsorship proposal template

We have included a **Sponsorship Proposal Template** on page 102 for you to use as a guideline. Clearly, you will need to adapt this to your own property and style but this should give you a good place to start. For best results, you may want to consider the following suggestions:

➤ You must include all of the information in the template in order for a sponsor to be able to make a decision.

➤ We prefer a proposal that breaks each of the proposal headings onto their own page or at least separates them clearly, keeping it easy and straightforward to read.

➤ Do not use an executive summary—your contact will tend to read that and not get to the meat of the proposal. Instead, use your cover letter to tell the contact very briefly what it is about and how it relates to them (see the **Proposal Cover Letter** on page 116).

➤ If you already have other sponsors committed, highlight this in your cover letter.

➤ If at all possible, include existing audience research.

➤ A major selling point for sponsors is that research will be done during the course of the sponsorship and provided to the sponsor, including at least a couple of questions provided by the sponsor. The perceived value of this to the sponsor is much higher than it may cost you. (See Chapter 5 for low-cost research strategies.)

➤ Create a proposal with an eye for detail and presentation. The more professional it looks, the more credible you are.

➤ Either comb bind your proposal or neatly staple it and enclose it in a presentation folder.

➤ Include such items as brochures, calendars of events and so on for review by the sponsor but do not make the sponsor search for pertinent information in these documents. If it is important (such as key dates, locations, etc.), it must be included in the proposal itself, ideally in the event details section.

➤ Do not send a video with your proposal. It wastes money and sponsors almost never look at them. If you are invited to make a presentation, you may want to show a video and then offer to leave a copy at that time if they want it for further review.

Confidentiality

Unfortunately, we have all heard of cases where a sponsee went to a company with a great idea for an event but was turned down, only to see their idea implemented directly by the company a few months or a year later. This is not the norm but it does make sense to protect your ideas.

If the proposal includes any of your creative ideas, it should include a legal statement that all concepts included are your property. A sample can be found below. This should be placed *before* the body of your proposal, such as at the bottom of your title page.

> © *Copyright* [organisation name] *1999. This publication is copyright and remains the intellectual property of* [organisation]. *No part of it may be reproduced by any means without the prior written permission of* [organisation].

Depending upon the confidentiality of it, you may also want to include this wording:

> *The information contained in this proposal is confidential and no part*
> *of it may be copied and/or disclosed to any person without the express*
> *permission of* [organisation].

Pricing

While developing your sponsorship proposal, you also need to address pricing. This is no doubt the most vexing area of creating a proposal and, unfortunately, we cannot offer any hard and fast rules. We can, however, offer a few strategies that should help.

First and foremost, the total fee must be less expensive than if the sponsor were to run the event on their own. The overall package must represent value for money.

Use your proposal to prove that what your organisation has to offer will benefit your potential sponsor more than the equivalent in above-the-line advertising. This must be substantially more—approximately 150–200 per cent more—because there is a tendency for corporations to stick to their comfort zone.

No matter what, never tell the potential sponsor how you are going to spend the money! This undermines your value and indicates your need rather than your worth. It also undermines the perception that you are a professional, viable organisation whether they participate or not. It is not unusual for a sponsor to request a breakdown of marketing and promotional expenditure.

Calculating your baseline fee

When calculating your price, you must firstly understand that a significant chunk of the sponsorship fee will go towards providing the promised benefits, as well as paying for the sale, servicing and administration of the sponsorship. The difference between those costs and the fee is your profit—the amount that you will actually be able to put towards increasing your revenue base.

> Cost of providing benefits offered
> + Staff and administration costs
> + Sales costs
> + Servicing costs
> _____
> = Your total cost

Once you have calculated the total cost of providing the sponsorship, you need to add in your profit. Your profit is the money you get to use as income to underwrite an event or program, or simply to add to your bottom line. As a rough

Never tell the potential sponsor how you are going to spend the money.

Remember, your baseline fee is *only* a baseline, not your final price.

guideline, your baseline fee will be approximately double your total cost, for a profit of 100 per cent.

Total cost to deliver the program

+ 100 per cent profit (revenue for your event)

= Your baseline fee

Once you know your baseline fee, you need to stack it up against market indicators. These indicators could show that you are in the right ballpark or, more likely, they could show that you are significantly under- or overpriced. If your baseline fee is overpriced against the market, you will have to readdress the benefits package and/or how it is delivered to ensure that it provides adequate income for your event. There is no use going to all the trouble to sell and service a sponsorship if it's not providing you with any benefit, or worse, if it costs you more to provide the sponsorship than you charge for the package.

Determining market price

Once you have determined your baseline fee, you need to adjust it to reflect the marketplace in which you operate. Ask yourself the following questions.

➤ What is the cost of similar sponsorship products on the market? Corporate sponsorship managers talk to each other and know the price of similar sponsorship packages. You need to have that same understanding.

➤ How does your product stand up? If similar events are offering the standard 'tickets and logo exposure' package and you are offering a turn-key solution, then you can promote your product as having a much higher value.

➤ How does your sponsorship servicing measure up? If you are constantly willing to go the extra mile to make a sponsorship work, then you will be consistently adding value to the package.

➤ Are there any other variables that might affect your price? What if your team wins the national championships? What if you lose your star player?

➤ How much is your potential sponsor likely to invest? Precedent is not always a reliable indicator but if you know a sponsor has never invested more than $20 000 in a sponsorship program and you are approaching them with a package valued at over $100 000, you need to understand that you will probably encounter some resistance. You will need to build a strong case for that level of investment, as well as possibly being prepared to negotiate for a lower level of benefits.

No sponsorship proposal should be valued solely on what you need to make the project work.

No sponsorship should be valued solely on what you need.

The above questions should get you pretty close to the market value of your event. In order to double check yourself, you should do the following:

➤ Pay attention to the marketplace—read sponsorship publications, join a sponsorship or marketing association, extend your network

➤ Use your network—we know people who won't send out a proposal without running it past three trusted colleagues first.

Equivalent opportunity cost

When calculating your price you also need to understand what you are competing against in terms of media—the 'equivalent opportunity cost' as media buyers put it.

If you are seeking money for a sponsorship, you need to understand how a sponsor *could* spend this money. You need to understand that you are not only competing with other sponsorship seekers but you are also competing with the main media, endorsements and sales promotions.

Remember that a sponsor will most likely support their sponsorship with at least one dollar (and often two or more dollars) for each dollar they spend on the sponsorship fee. If you are asking for $50 000, you can be assured that they are looking at it as an investment of $100 000–$150 000. You should calculate the equivalent opportunity cost based upon their total investment, not just your fee.

Questions you need to ask to determine how else a sponsor could be spending their money include:

➤ How many television commercials could they buy in peak viewing with that investment?

➤ How many black and white pages in metropolitan daily newspapers?

➤ How many colour pages in mainstream or targeted magazines?

➤ How many weeks of 30-second spots, at a rate of thirty per week, on metropolitan radio?

➤ How many billboards?

You should be able to get these costs from your advertising agency or media placement company. If you don't have either of these, you will need to secure price lists from key media throughout your marketplace and make an educated estimate.

If your event or program is national in scope, get national figures. If it is limited to one city or region, then get figures specific to that region. And remember to use figures that are representative of the discounts given to large advertisers, not casual rates, which will be much higher.

In addition to giving you an understanding of your competitive position, knowing what a sponsor could get for their investment can really help you during the sales process, particularly if your event or program offers strong benefits over time.

Imagine being able to make a case for your highly targeted, strongly matched two-month event, offering a whole range of benefits to meet the sponsor's objectives versus them placing five advertisements during '60 Minutes'. Used judiciously, this can be a very powerful argument but you must be absolutely confident in the value of your offer.

Proposal issues

There are a number of issues that come up over and over again around the creation and presentation of sponsorship proposals. We have addressed some of the most common ones here.

Should we offer different sponsorship levels?

A lot of sponsorship seekers offer levels to their potential sponsors—gold, silver and bronze levels are very popular (and overused to the point of being a cliché). The main problem with this approach is that, without realising it, most sponsees formulate the packages so that all of the levels get access to the best benefits, with the main difference being that the lower levels get less of the supporting benefits.

Clearly, this is not an approach that is conducive to creating strong, high-level sponsorships. It undermines the true value of the relationship, creating instead a bargain hunter's paradise.

At the same time, everyone likes choice, including sponsors. So the trick is working out how to offer sponsors a choice without undermining your value and potential revenue. We have identified two good ways around this: 'The apple and orange approach' and 'The up-selling approach'.

The apple and orange approach

This approach revolves around the strategy of offering two packages that are completely different from each other, each emphasising a differing set of sponsor objectives. You don't want the potential sponsor to be able to compare them on a benefit-for-benefit basis, so you create an apple and an orange. Ideally, the packages should be priced similarly, but even if they aren't, this strategy can work very well.

This is very different from the above 'levels' strategy of offering three different-sized apples. If all the potential sponsor wants is an apple, they will almost certainly take the smallest, cheapest one.

The following is a very generalised example of two packages that a basketball team could offer to a potential confectionery sponsor—same sponsee, same sponsor but very different outcomes.

Offer 1: emphasis on VIP hospitality

➤ Naming rights to team mascot

➤ Use of private box (seating twelve) for eight featured games

➤ Autographed team merchandise for all sponsor guests

➤ Post-game player meet and greets in the box for each game (one or two players, as available), as well as team mascot

➤ Inclusion of VIP's children in half-time activities (as appropriate)

➤ Thirty pairs of premium tickets to other games

➤ VIP tickets and travel for six to an all-star game

Offer 2: emphasis on new product launch

➤ Naming rights to team mascot

➤ Naming rights to a feature game

➤ Media launch for new product at the game

➤ Attendance at launch by coach and mascot

➤ Half-time on-court product launch stunt and audience contest

➤ Exit sampling of new product for all attendees of launch game

➤ Use of hospitality room for VIP guests at featured game (seating fifty)

➤ Consumer raffle boxes located around venue

➤ Twenty-four pairs of reserved seat tickets to future games for use in consumer raffles

The up-selling approach

Another strategy that we favour is offering one highly tailored package, with an optional upgrade available at extra cost. Our experience is that, in a high percentage of cases, once the potential sponsor is sold on the concept of a partnership with a sponsee, they look at the upgrade as an opportunity to maximise the sponsorship and take it up.

Do remember to go through the pricing exercise for both the offer and the upgrade to ensure that you are covering all of your costs.

Below, we have provided an example of the offer and upgrade prepared by the same basketball team to the same confectionery company potential sponsor.

Sponsorship offer

➤ Naming rights to team mascot

➤ Naming rights to a feature game

➤ Media launch for new product at the game

➤ Attendance at launch by coach and mascot

➤ Half-time on-court product launch stunt and audience contest

➤ Exit sampling of new product for all attendees of launch game

➤ Use of hospitality room for VIP guests at featured game (seating fifty)

➤ Post-game player meet and greet in the hospitality room (one or two players, as available), as well as team mascot

➤ Consumer raffle boxes located around venue

➤ Twenty-four pairs of reserved seat tickets to future games for use in consumer raffles

Optional VIP hospitality upgrade

➤ Use of private box (seating twelve) for six additional featured games

➤ Inclusion of VIP's children in half-time activities (as appropriate)

➤ VIP tickets and travel for six to an all-star game

Do we need a glossy sales brochure or video?

Unfortunately, when it comes to selling sponsorship, a lot of sponsees rely on flash over-substance. They produce glossy sales brochures outlining the sponsorship packages (often laid out in levels). While these brochures are often beautifully prepared, they lack what sponsors want most—customisation.

Rather than going to the effort and expense to create slick sales materials, put that effort into researching your potential sponsors and creating highly customised proposals. Every one of the sponsors we have polled has supported this contention. Your proposal should be neat and professional—do put it on letterhead and bind it. That is all the sponsor expects from the presentation.

What is useful to sponsors is providing examples of all of your event promotional materials from previous years, if you have them. If not, you could include one or two mock-ups of the planned materials for the current event. This will showcase the style and degree of professionalism that your organisation has, as well as add colour to the presentation.

Do you need a video? In a word, no. Sponsors never watch them—most sponsorship managers have a shelf full of videos they have never seen. And if you bring one along with you to your meeting, you can be virtually assured that something will go wrong with the audiovisual. A well-planned and enthusiastic verbal presentation will give you a lot more mileage.

Photographs and diagrams are a different story. If your event is extremely visual, such as an art exhibition, photographs are a must. If your event is an expo of some type, a map or other diagram will give the sponsor an opportunity to understand your vision and their place in it.

Should we go to one company at a time or can we go to several?

In a perfect world, you would only go to one company in any given product category at a time. But, as you have already gathered from reading this book, creating relationships takes time. You are highly unlikely to have enough lead time before your event to research, approach and negotiate your sponsorships using this approach.

In reality, it is perfectly alright to have several offers out at one time. If you have done your background research, this should not exceed ten or twelve companies and the offers will most likely be very different from each other, reflecting the different needs of the various companies.

How much lead time does a potential sponsor need?

Most sponsors set their larger sponsorship expenditures as part of their marketing budget, twelve to eighteen months before the events. They will often have an additional amount of money set aside for opportunistic spending if something else comes up. This amount is usually, but not always, fairly limited and will not accommodate major sponsorships. Only if something really extraordinary comes along will they breach this plan.

In addition, companies need time to maximise sponsorships. Usually, the more product lines, customer types, distribution channels and so on that they have, the longer it will take them to make the most of their sponsorships. This should be as important to you as it is to them because a happy sponsor is a good sponsor.

It is imperative that you ask the question about lead times when doing your background research on potential sponsors. Only then will you know for sure what their policy is. As a very rough guideline, we have found the following time frames to be common across a lot of companies.

18–24 months

➤ Major sponsorships (often national and/or televised)
➤ Multinational sponsorships
➤ Multi-year events

12–18 months

Most sponsorships come under this time frame

6–12 months

If you go below twelve months, you may still have some success at creating major sponsorship relationships. Most likely, however, you will start having to undercut the value of the sponsorship because the sponsor won't have time to maximise the program fully. You will also start running into budget problems and may have to get creative with pricing and payments.

If you are looking for a smaller investment (under $100 000 or so), you can often have success without undercutting your value right down to six months.

If you have missed the budgeting time frame, you will probably be accessing a limited pool of opportunistic funds. You can sometimes increase your chances by going directly to the product marketing areas, as they often have opportunistic funds that are not specific to sponsorship and can make decisions with a somewhat shorter lead time if they can be directly tied to product objectives.

Under 6 months

These investments are reserved for surprise or unanticipated events.

Unanticipated events are events such as a major sporting team winning the championships. Around that one unanticipated event, a wide range of other sponsorable events could crop up. These are the only type of events that we recommend sponsors should consider with less than six months' lead time.

If you are trying to sell sponsorship for a planned event with less than six months' lead time, you are extremely unlikely to be successful. Not only do you hit obstacles such as the sponsor not having enough time to maximise the sponsorship or the budget already being set, but it also smacks of desperation and could undermine your credibility as a strong and highly sponsorable organisation for years.

When is the best time to approach sponsors?

The best time to approach a potential sponsor is before they have set the marketing budget for the year in which your event or organisation is seeking sponsorship. It is as simple as that. Again, you need to ask the question of the potential sponsor when you are doing your preliminary research—well before providing them with a proposal.

There is one timing long shot that you can try, however. If you have a smaller sponsorship on offer, you may want to approach a potential sponsor within six to eight weeks of the end of the financial year. If they have any unspent funds in their sponsorship budget for that year, you may be able to access them. Extra funds are usually as a result of the above-mentioned opportunistic budget not being fully utilised over the course of the year.

▌Sponsorship proposal template

Sales4.doc

1

Australiana Airways
and
The Sydney International
Fishing Expo

Date

Use your own judgment when doing the title page, but do show the sponsor name and your name together using the word 'and' or 'presents' or, if you are selling the naming rights, show the name of the event as it would be if they took up the sponsorship. Always date your proposal and always put it on nice lettterhead.

2

'The worst day fishing is better than the best day working'

Anonymous

Use this page to set the stage. We like using a relevant quote— funny, inspirational, or something that just says it all. Your challenge is to really get to the core of what your event is about— the beauty of flowers, the spirit of competition, the dignity of the underprivileged. Buy a good quote book and use it.

If your event is very visual, a colour copy of something relatively simple—one flower, a pair of dancers—can be very powerful, on its own or with a quote. Use the facilities of a scanner or colour copier to crop in your photo to a manageable size.

Give a good overview of what this event is about and how being involved will benefit the sponsor. At this point in the proposal, your appeal is basically emotional. You want your target to be able to visualise the event and how their involvement will look and feel.

Use emotional wording—a lot of strong adjectives (get a thesaurus).

As a general rule, two-thirds of this page should be devoted to visualising the event, and the remainder to visualising the sponsorship.

3

Overview

In November 1999, the Darling Harbour Convention Centre will throw open its doors and welcome 65 000 enthusiastic fishermen and women to the Sydney International Fishing Expo.

They will be treated to over 100 demonstrations and activities for all types and levels of experience. They will enjoy over 450 exhibitors from Australia and overseas and will have the opportunity to try out their gear on the largest indoor trout lake in the world. And as high consumers of fishing tourism, they will flock to our brand new Fishing Adventures area and can even book their trips on-site.

Approximately 40% of Australian men fish at least once a year, with a quarter of them fishing at least once a month. These men love their sport and they make sure that they are equipped for it to be as successful and enjoyable as possible. On average, these fishermen and women spend over $150 each at the Expo.

Where does Australiana fit in? Based upon our visitor survey last year, over 65% of fishermen fly to a fishing destination at least once every two years, with the average size of their group being 4–6. This is broken down very evenly between overseas and rural Australian destinations, allowing Australiana to showcase not only major international destinations, but your extensive regional network as well.

As a major sponsor of the Sydney International Fishing Expo and naming-rights sponsor to our new travel area, Australiana Fishing Adventures, complete with exclusive on-site booking facilities, Australiana will enjoy a major profile with this lucrative market. You will also have the platform to create meaningful promotions, cementing the relationship with these consumers, tourist boards, adventure travel specialists, and travel agents.

4

Event details

Dates and times:	Friday, 12 November 1999, 1:00–10:00 p.m. Saturday, 13 November, 10:00 a.m.–6:00 p.m. Sunday, 14 November, 10:00 a.m.–6:00 p.m.
Location:	Darling Harbour Convention Centre, Sydney
Attendees:	We are targeting 65 000 attendees over the three-day show. This is a projected 5% increase on 1998. Attendance has increased by an average of 5% over each of the past five years.
Target demographics:	Our primary demographic target is males 18–35. The secondary demographic is males 35–50. A comprehensive breakdown of target markets and an overview of recent audience research is attached.
Cost:	$12 adults, $5 for children under 12, $30 for a family of four. This is consistent with charges for similar shows and reflects a $1 increase on the adult fee from 1998.
Parking and transportation:	There are 5000 parking spots at the Convention Centre ramp. In addition, we have arranged for a free shuttle bus service from the Casino parking ramp. The Convention Centre is accessible by bus and light rail, as well as by ferry from Circular Quay.

This is where you list the hard information about the event. Be straightforward and completely unemotional. This will not only answer a lot of questions your target sponsor may have, but is also your opportunity to show how organised you are.

5

Target audience

Based upon audience research (attached), our media and promotional campaign is aimed directly at the following demographic and psychographic groups.

1. Fishing enthusiasts—people from all walks of life that fish more than twenty times per year. Based on audience research, these people make up 13% of our audience, and accounted for 37% of all product sales in 1998.
2. Up and coming males aged 28–45, who generally take one major fishing trip per year, generally travelling in groups of 4–6. Low consumers of fishing products, high consumers of fishing tourism. These people make up 5% of our audience, and average $3200 per year expenditure on fishing tourism.
3. Males 18–35, occasional to regular fishermen, tend to fish in groups of family or friends, see fishing as a quality time activity for families, and in particular, to bond with their children.
4. Males 35+, regular fishermen, generally fathers/grandfathers, similar psychographic to above.
5. Other markets—people who would rather go to a show than stay home, fathers who need to entertain the kids for a weekend, people whose existing plans are cancelled by bad weather.

As with the previous five years, we will be embarking upon comprehensive market research again in 1999. We are happy to include up to four travel-related questions on Australiana's behalf and will provide Australiana with the full results of the research.

If the sponsor's primary target market is your secondary or tertiary target market, be sure to emphasise the marketplace(s) that are most relevant to them.

If hospitality it is a major factor in the package, outline all hospitality opportunities here. If it is a minor factor, move this back towards the benefits section.

If on-site sales, preferred vending status, or product demonstration is a big factor, you will also want to include a section on sales, vending, and display in this area of your proposal.

7

On-site activities

A number of on-site activities will have major impact for Australiana, including both hospitality and on-site sales.

Hospitality

On Saturday night, 13 November, we will be throwing a travel agents-only cocktail party in the Australiana Fishing Adventures area. Australiana will be promoted as the host of this party and you are welcome to invite up to 100 agents on top of the 250 core adventure travel specialists identified by the Expo.

A number of our celebrities and demonstrators will be on-hand to discuss these destinations with agents. A feature will be a fishing 'tournament' where agents will compete for a number of travel prizes by casting their line into the trout lake (it borders the Australiana Fishing Adventures area). To keep it light, prizes will be awarded for biggest fish, smallest fish, prettiest fish, most stylish cast, etc.

Finally, as part of your package, we will provide Australiana with 2500 double passes to the Expo, so that you can provide added value to your core business travellers.

On-site sales

As naming-rights sponsor to the Australiana Fishing Adventures area, you will be located in a large, central area, themed to resemble a fishing cabin. Arrangements have been made to provide this area with power and other cabling necessary to run an Australiana reservations area on-site. Australiana will be the exclusive air travel company represented at the Expo.

As this is the first year for the Australiana Fishing Adventures area, there is little direct precedent, but similar areas at the Great Adventure Sports Expo and Harbour Golf Show have resulted in on-site bookings valued at between $6–8 per attendee. At a projected 65 000 attendees, this equates to on-site sales valued at between $390 000–520 000.

To ensure the greatest possible opportunity for Australiana to develop travel packages with our other travel exhibitors, we will provide Australiana with an exhibitor list and contact details no later than eight weeks prior to the Expo.

Write one paragraph outlining your television advertising and promotion, as well as any sponsorship deals you have with a television station that might increase the value of your media further. Be sure to note what is and is not confirmed. Do not mislead your sponsors. Take the same approach for each media vehicle

6

Media support

Based upon target market research, we have created a media plan that will generate interest in and awareness of the Expo, while specifically targeting our key markets.

Our total budget for paid and promotional media is $150 000, and with that we have been able to negotiate $450 000 in media value. A full media schedule and an audience profile are attached in the Appendix.

Television

Our comprehensive television campaign focuses on two main areas:

- Two four-week media promotions, run in conjunction with Channel 8 programs 'Lon Davies' Fishing World' and 'Great Vacations'. 'Fishing World' reaches 100 000 avid fishermen and women in the greater Sydney area every week. 'Great Vacations', Channel 8's new vacation program, reaches 350 000 people, mainly active travellers, each week.
- Paid media schedule on Channel 8, supported by tactical advertising on Channels 7 and 10. These schedules will run for four weeks prior to and through the Sydney International Fishing Expo.

Radio

We have negotiated a three-week drive-time promotional schedule on 2UW running prior to and through the Expo. The schedule is anchored by a major fishing vacation promotion. This station matches our core audience profiles almost exactly.

This schedule will be augmented by two-week limited schedules on NNN and 2SS, reinforcing the messages on the other two stations most listened to by our audience and ensuring that we get the most complete coverage of our key markets in the lead-up to the Expo.

Newspaper

The Sydney International Fishing Expo is sponsored by the *Sydney Mirror*. As part of that partnership, we have negotiated a series of five advertisements per week, including 1/6th page ads in the Friday What's On section and page-dominant ads in the Saturday Travel section.

Magazines

We are embarking upon a limited magazine campaign, with placements in *Ralph* and *Fish Lover*'s magazines.

Other event promotion

In addition to paid and promotional media, we will embark upon a comprehensive publicity and non-media promotional campaign.

Publicity

We have engaged the services of one of the country's top publicists, [*insert publicist or company name*], who have designed a campaign targeting both general and niche media. This campaign will kick off with a media launch on 27 October and will continue through the Expo.

We will be providing media access to top experts and celebrities, including Lon Davies and the cast of *Great Vacations* for interviews, photos, and expert commentary.

As this is the first year for the Australiana Fishing Adventures area, we will be concentrating a large portion of our publicity effort on the promotion of this part of the Expo. Australiana will benefit greatly from the promotion of travel destinations and packages, a key part of this strategy.

We are also very happy to assist Australiana in developing a publicity plan that targets your specific consumer and intermediary markets.

Signage

For two weeks prior to the Expo, and running through the Expo, ten vertical flags will be featured around the Darling Harbour area. During that period, the Expo will also be promoted on the Convention Centre's electronic billboard.

Web site

We have a year round Web site, generating 480 000 hits annually, with 35% of those hits in the month prior to the Expo. The Web site includes a wide variety of information about the show, its sponsors, and exhibitors, and is featured on all appropriate media promotion and publicity.

Direct mail

As we have a strong Internet presence, we conduct our direct mail using e-mail to the 88 000 people who have requested notification and early ticket booking. We will be contacting them, including a link to our site, six weeks prior to the Expo and again two weeks prior.

8

Suggested promotional overlays

As fishing travel correlates strongly with business travellers, we suggest the following promotions to make this partnership relevant to your key customers.

Australiana Club promotion

We suggest that you run a simple enter-to-win promotion for your highest-value customers, members of the Australiana Club. As these members are generally in the higher socioeconomic bracket, it would be important to ensure that entry is easy and the perceived value of the prizes is high.

The grand prize-winner would receive a group fishing package for six to an exotic international location. The Cook Islands Tourist Board has expressed interest in providing hotel accommodation and daily top-level fishing trips (both deep sea and inland) if you think this destination is appropriate for your core customers.

A second prize-winner would receive a group fishing package for four to one of Australia's top regional fishing destinations. Again, the Snowy Mountain Tourism Council has agreed to provide lodge accommodation, meals, and fishing trips, including a full day at a destination so remote it can only be reached by helicopter. If you would prefer to feature another destination, we are happy to work with you to arrange the ground portion of the package.

2500 third prize-winners will receive a complimentary double pass to the Sydney International Fishing Expo (provided as part of your sponsorship package).

Entry will be in Australiana Club lounges, and could be as simple as swiping their Club membership cards (as you did last year for the Indy Car promotion).

Fishing travel features

We strongly suggest that you utilise this sponsorship across your range of customer publications, including *Australiana Club News*, your Frequent Flyer newsletter, and your in-flight publication, *Go Australiana*. These could feature a range of subjects, including:

* fishing destination profiles and specials
* fishing tips from our experts
* fishing-oriented promotions
* how to pack your fishing gear for air travel.

We will provide all required assistance to develop content for these publications and have a number of exhibitors who are already interested in advertising and/or developing co-promotions with you.

We have only provided a sampling of the benefits that might go along with this package–ideally, this list should be at least a couple of pages long. Use your inventory and create a comprehensive list of real benefits. Depending upon how long the list is, you may want to categorise the benefits (like the inventory).

A hint to all of you–logo exposure is only a small fraction of a good benefits package.

This package must, must, must be customised to your sponsor's needs.

This area is optional but, if you have done your homework on the sponsor, is your opportunity to solve their problems and/or meet their needs.

For instance, you could...

* *tell the airline how it can give incentives to their frequent flyers or VIP lounge members*
* *tell the brewer how it can run promotions in pubs for free merchandise and tickets*
* *tell the cereal company how it can use your event to get into schools*
* *tell the insurance company how it can support the launch of their new product*
* *tell the mobile phone company how it can capture potential customer details and the age of their current telephones (for replacement)*
* *and so on.*

Brainstorm with your staff. Do a lot of research on precedents, both national and international, as there is a wealth of information about what works and there is no reason why you need to reinvent the wheel.

9

Benefits

As a major sponsor of the Sydney International Fishing Expo and naming-rights sponsor of the Australiana Fishing Adventures area, you will receive the following comprehensive package of benefits:

Sponsorship

* naming-rights sponsorship of the Australiana fishing adventures area, incorporating the Australiana logo in all signage and promotional material
* major sponsorship of the Sydney International Fishing Show (we are limited to three major sponsors)
* official airline partner status
* sponsorship and sales exclusivity in the category of air travel

On-site

* 10 m × 10 m site in prime, central location in the Fishing Adventures area. This site has a themed 'fishing cabin' structure on it and is fully cabled for computers and telephone access
* opportunity to book air travel and packages on site
* logo acknowledgment on all 'Sydney International Fishing Expo' signage

Hospitality and networking

* host status for Saturday evening travel agent cocktail party
* ability to invite up to 100 additional travel agents (on top of the 250 adventure travel specialists we have already identified)
* introduction to all Fishing Adventures exhibitors a minimum of eight weeks prior to the Expo
* facilitation of travel cross-promotions and packages with other exhibitors

Media profile

* use of Australiana as an intrinsic part of all travel-oriented publicity activities (promoting travel packages, destinations, on-site booking, etc.)
* logo/name inclusion in all paid and promotional media and publicity
* assistance with developing and implementing a publicity plan for Australiana's key marketplaces

Tickets

* 25 VIP passes to the Expo
* 8 VIP car parking spaces
* 2500 adult double passes to the Expo, for use in promoting the Expo to your business travel customers

Outline how much this is going to cost in cash and contra. Be sure to include a proposed payment schedule. We also like to include a minimum promotional commitment, ensuring that they embark upon at least some activities to maximise the sponsorship, and that they are activities that will benefit you, the sponsorship seeker, as well.

10

Investment

Your investment for this comprehensive sponsorship relationship will be:

- $90 000 cash
- $5000 domestic air travel for use by event staff (to be used by 31 December 1999)
- Provision of return air travel for two to Bali, for use as a drawing prize facilitating our audience research (full credit for the prize will be given to Australiana)
- Provision of return air travel for two to Darwin, for use as the major prize for our promotion on 2UW (full credit for the prize will be given to Australiana)
- Commitment to strongly promote the Sydney International Fishing Expo to your Australiana Club members and frequent flyers, as well as in *Go Australiana* magazine

Half of the cash component will be due upon signing a contract, with the remainder due on 1 September 1999. The entire domestic air travel fund should be made available to the Sydney International Fishing Expo upon signing the contract.

Chapter 7

Sales process

Sales checklist

You have done your research, the sponsor is interested and there's no spinach in your teeth—it must be time for a meeting!

Prepare, prepare, prepare

It has been suggested that the sales process is 75 per cent preparation, 10 per cent sales pitch and 15 per cent follow-up. If you have the opportunity to meet the sponsor in person, ensure that you know everything you can possibly find out about their company before you walk through the door. You need to know what matters to your potential sponsors and how they measure success. Are they after sales opportunities, launching a new product, preparing for a share issue or embarking on any of a myriad of other marketing activities?

Determine what you want to achieve from this meeting

Ideally, your initial meeting should be about gathering and confirming information. Both you and the potential sponsor want information. You want to create a customised proposal that addresses your sponsor's specific marketing objectives and you need to expand on what you know in order to deliver an appropriate offer. On the other side, your potential sponsor wants to know about you and your event. Your counterpart will be asking you a few key questions:

➤ Who are you and why should I do business with you?

➤ What's unique about this event and can it deliver the target markets I want?

➤ Why will people come to your event?

➤ What's in it for me?

➤ How much is it going to cost me?

It will increase your credibility exponentially if you can answer all of these questions before the sponsor asks them. You should be able to sum up your event, your expertise and your enthusiasm concisely, providing the key information to your potential sponsor, so that you can then get on with your own information gathering.

Check your vocabulary

It is important in sales meetings to talk the corporate language. This reminds your corporate contacts that you think like they do—in business terms. Start substituting corporate terms for terms that are often used by smaller sponsees and non-profit organisations (see below).

INSTEAD OF...	USE
'Awareness', 'exposure' or 'profile'	'Opportunity to communicate your marketing message'
'Small audience' or 'small audience of enthusiasts'	'Highly targeted' or 'pure demographic'
'Support'	'Invest'
'Cost' or 'fee'	'Investment'
'Donation' or 'gift'	'Investment'
'Donor', 'funder' or 'supporter'	'Investor', 'sponsor' or 'partner'
'Reaching a small audience'	'Narrowcasting' (the opposite of broadcasting)
'Surplus' (extra funds)	'Profit'
'Marketing dollars'	'Sponsorship' or 'Investment'

Instead of 'awareness', 'exposure' or 'profile', use 'opportunity to communicate your marketing message'.

Make contact with the right person

Establish who you should contact and make an appointment to see him or her. Ensure you meet with someone who has the authority to make decisions on sponsorships of your size.

Mind your manners

Be on time and keep the meeting on track and on schedule. Speak with confidence, smile and shake hands firmly. Speak clearly and remember you are there to gather and check information. Remember, you have two ears and one mouth for a reason—you need to listen twice as much as you speak. Whatever you do, don't go into hyper sales mode. And be sure to follow up the meeting with a personal thank you note (see sample on page 118).

If you are a non-profit organisation, make it clear that you are not looking for a donation

Ensure that your contact knows that you are not asking for a donation because this will often be their assumption. It will be even more imperative for you to be very businesslike, using business vocabulary, and discussing the project in terms of it being an investment.

Always focus on the sponsor's needs

Remember as you talk that these people are not interested in meeting your needs but in achieving their own business objectives.

Don't discuss price

Do not talk about the price until after you have excited them about the idea. Avoid setting your price until after the initial meeting. It is acceptable to discuss a price range or an indicative amount but always follow that with the caveat that it is only an indication and that the fee will be set based upon the benefits package offered as a result of the meeting.

Be enthusiastic

Your enthusiasm is your greatest selling tool. Following the meeting, send a thank you letter outlining what you have discussed, answering any questions and indicating when they will receive your formal proposal.

Using a broker

No one can sell your organisation or its products the way you can. However, if your organisation lacks the skills, experience or the resources to sell your sponsorship property, hire a broker.

What to look for in a broker or an agent

Experience

Ensure your broker or agent supplies you with a list of clients (including the specific events or properties s/he has acted as a broker for), amounts raised for each, how long the sales processes took and references. If you are working with a larger sales agency, be sure to get references on both the agency and the specific person or team handling your event.

Understanding of the product

Does your broker understand and empathise with your project? Has s/he worked with similar properties?

Value added

Determine exactly what your broker will and will not do. A good broker will work with you to ensure the property, marketing plan and the offer work for potential sponsors.

Professional affiliations

Is s/he a member of at least one recognised sponsorship or marketing association?

Exclusivity

No sponsorship brokers worth their salt will handle a property unless they have exclusive selling rights. Tag teams are bad for them and bad for you. Have they insisted on exclusivity? For how long? It is not uncommon for a broker to request a period of three to twelve months for the securing of sponsorship.

Hunger

How hungry is your sponsorship broker? A good broker is hungry for the project. Is yours?

Presentation

How does your broker present him or herself? Is s/he professional? What are his/her meeting and presentation skills like?

How s/he works

Ask how s/he sells properties. What is his/her strategy and philosophy? If s/he takes an uncustomised, shotgun approach to sales, don't use him/her.

Marketing and business knowledge

Many brokers specialise in particular areas—sports, events, arts, community. Find out the areas of specialisation. Who are his/her contacts? What are his/her networks?

Follow-up and reporting

At the beginning of the contract period, establish how frequently you want the broker to report back, what information you need and in what format.

Fees and payments

Brokers work on a commission basis with the fees ranging anywhere from 10–30 per cent or even more. Brokers are paid only if they successfully negotiate the sponsorship on your behalf. Brokers are responsible for producing their own sales material. However, if you want flash brochures, videos and whiz bang presentation materials, you will be expected to cover production and printing costs. Also, you need to be clear on whether the commission is to be paid from the total amount sought or added to it. For example, if they are raising $100 000, are you paying them $20 000 of the $100 000 they raise or do they have to raise $120 000 to cover their own commission? The latter is becoming much more common and is usually more desirable for you.

Contracts and letters of agreement

Ensure you have one. The contract should include commission payable, reporting deadlines, clearances and sign offs, exclusions, time frame and amount sought. Also, be sure to include whether the commission is to be added to the total amount sought or paid from it.

Consulting assistance

If you need assistance determining the nature of the property, pricing and packaging or assistance in managing the sponsorship, the broker will charge an hourly fee or a project fee for these services. Fees range from $150 to $300 per hour.

Where to find brokers

Personal referrals are best. If you don't know anyone that uses or has used a broker, call your local marketing or sponsorship association and ask for a referral.

Preliminary letter

Letter1.doc

26 June 1999

Mr Brian Doe
Managing Director
ARN Australia Pty Limited
Unit A, 108 McEvoy St
Waterloo NSW 2017

Dear Mr Doe,

I am writing to introduce the School Administrators Federation (SAF), to tell you about its services and to invite you to consider a sponsorship proposal.

When decisions affecting education and school administration are made, it is the SAF's business to understand all the issues involved. The Federation has unrivalled access to all aspects of Australia's school administration system, bringing together the interests of those who manage schools, those who work in them, those who design and build them and those who supply them with goods and services.

SAF is a non-profit national industry association of school administrators. Founded in 1989, SAF works to enhance the quality of school administration for public and private schools across the nation.

The Federation is recognised by governments, educational professionals and the teaching community as a national leader in the school administration industry and is well placed to give you access to all the important networks relevant to your marketing needs.

Our regular activities include:

➤ Annual Conference of School Administrators—our national conference brings together teachers, administrators, policy makers, purchasing officers and suppliers. The 1999 Conference is to be held at the Adelaide Convention Exhibition Centre from Friday, 12 November to Tuesday, 16 November.

➤ Seminars—Administration Workshops and Financial Management and Purchasing Seminars are held throughout the year and enjoy sell-out attendance with over 15 000 participants annually.

➤ Publications—SAF produces a newsletter, Schools Administrator Today and an Education Administrator paper, Head of the Class, every quarter. Circulation for our publications is over 120 000.

➤ Awards—SAF recognises and encourages innovation and excellence in school administration with the National School Administrator of the Year awards.

➤ Industry Information—SAF has access to a wide range of up-to-date national and international school administrator information and can assist suppliers, policy makers and educational professionals with industry research requests. We maintain an active database of over 25 000 purchasing officers and school administrators.

At SAF, we are committed to creating and maintaining win–win partnerships with industry suppliers. We have a number of sponsorship opportunities ranging from sales and exhibition properties to exclusive conference packages.

I have included a brochure on SAF for your interest.

I will ring your offices on Tuesday morning to discuss your specific marketing and sponsorship objectives and how we might tailor a proposal for you.

Sincerely,

Kate Beldar-Phillips
Marketing Manager

Proposal cover letter

Letter2.doc

15 January 1999

Karen Lansdown
Marketing Director
Acme Toy Company
17 Smith Street
Auckland, New Zealand

Dear Karen,

Thank you for inviting me to discuss your sponsorship marketing objectives. I enjoyed our meeting and feel confident that we have developed a sponsorship proposal to meet both your immediate and long-term needs.

Your situation

A brief overview of what where they are at and what they want.

Your objectives

As a result of our meeting, I have assessed that the specific sponsorship marketing objectives for your organisation are to:

➤   briefly list specific objectives in dot points.

The project/event

Provide a brief overview of the project.

Marketing and promotional benefits

Provide a very brief overview of the type and value of benefits.

Investment

Your investment in [event] will be repaid many times over as a result of your organisation's improved ability to identify and cultivate [clients, customers, sales].

The next step

I have attached a detailed proposal for [event]. Included in this document are the media advertising strategy and the public relations and promotional strategies.

Thank you once again for the chance to submit this proposal. We look forward to exploring a partnership with you and hope that we will have the opportunity to contribute to the success of your organisation over the long term.

Sincerely yours,

Jessica Marie Devaney
Sponsorship Director

Meeting thank you letter

Letter3.doc

26 August 1999

Adrian McMahon
Sponsorship Manager
Positively Vodka Importers
17–23 Longbridge Street
Sydney NSW 2001

Dear Adrian,

Thank you for taking time from your busy schedule to meet with me today to discuss your marketing objectives and your sponsorship guidelines.

The Woolloomooloo Theatre Company is committed to producing contemporary theatre productions that reflect our audiences' expectations. We are a contemporary, cutting edge company producing Australian theatre for Australian audiences. Like Positively Vodka, we are committed to building new audiences through carefully targeted sampling programs.

I am confident that a partnership with the Woolloomooloo Theatre Company will benefit both our organisations. Our upcoming subscription campaign targeting younger executives and opinion leaders provides a great opportunity for Positively Vodka to promote its newest range of flavoured vodkas.

I will forward a formal proposal to you on Friday. Thank you again for taking the time to meet with me today.

Yours sincerely,

Clint Manton
Marketing Manager

Rejection thank you letter

Letter4.doc

23 February 1999

Karen Lansdown
Marketing Director
Acme Toy Company
17 Smith Street
Sydney NSW 2001

Dear Karen,

I appreciate your having taken the time to review our proposal.

As you might expect, I am disappointed that Acme Toy cannot sponsor our PQR project. As we discussed, our PQR project provides unique marketing and promotional opportunities and access to your target markets in a cost-effective and creative manner. However, we recognise that it is impossible for you to invest in every potential sponsorship proposal.

I would very much like to keep in touch with you. We are currently developing a range of projects that are specifically targeting young families with toddlers and I feel confident that your marketing objectives can be addressed with one of our upcoming projects.

Thank you again for your considering our proposal.

Yours sincerely,

Robert D'Onofrio
General Manager

Chapter 8

Negotiation

The object of the negotiation process is to strike a win–win deal for all parties involved. In order to achieve this level of partnership, both parties must be completely open about their objectives. This should be a fairly straightforward task if the development of the offer were done in a fully collaborative manner, as recommended throughout this book.

Either way, there are a number of rules that will make negotiating sponsorship a lot easier for you.

NEGOTIATE PEER TO PEER

Negotiate peer to peer

Be sure you actually carry out the negotiation with someone who has the authority to negotiate and the ability to approve the expenditure. You will find that, in many companies, different levels of marketing executives will have different levels of financial authority.

Know your bottom line

In the heat of a meeting, it is easy to get caught up in the process and make a deal that you realise later does not achieve your financial objectives.

Before you go into any negotiation, be sure to do your homework. Go back to your pricing exercises and set yourself a bottom limit that you will under no circumstances fall below (e.g. 225 per cent of your cost to deliver the program). You may also want to set yourself a limit as to how much of the fee you will accept in contra.

Have something up your sleeve

When you create an offer for a sponsor, always keep a couple of nice benefits up your sleeve to use during the negotiation process. If you plan from the start to negotiate by offering them more, rather than settling for less money (and calculate your costs accordingly), you will end up far better off in the end.

Don't be bullied

Some sponsors routinely offer 20–25 per cent less than your asking price, assuming that if you are hungry enough, you will be grateful for anything. Don't fall for this ploy.

You need to approach the negotiation from a position of confidence—you are holding a negotiation, not a fire sale. You've done your research and know your value. If they have a problem with the price point, then you need to adjust your package accordingly. Do not ever simply accept a discounted offer. A sponsor worth working with will respect your need to protect the value of your property.

If you have approached the sponsorship process in a fully professional manner and taken all of the above negotiation advice, and the potential sponsor is still treating you like a second-class organisation, walk away because the relationship will never get any better.

Stay composed no matter what

Negotiations can be difficult, no question about it. Even if you have created a strong offer and followed the guidelines set out here, sometimes you will work with a sponsor who is an old-style negotiator, approaching the process as adversarial rather than collaborative.

If things start heating up, call for time out. Tell the potential sponsor that it is clear you both need to give this relationship a fresh look. Tell them that you will rework the offer, taking into account their concerns, and that you will get back to them in a couple of days. Then do it. Put any defensiveness or acrimony aside and find a way. Put the new offer in writing, which allows you to think it out fully, and remember to stay focused on a solution.

Also note, there may be times when a sponsorship negotiation will turn sour even when both sides are working together—as the result of an international directive, a change in business climate or because of an internal change at the company. Don't hold this against the potential sponsor as it is out of their control. Just stay composed and stay in touch, and when everything settles back down for them, resume discussions.

Be prepared to walk away

Don't ever walk into a negotiation with the mindset that you need to close the deal. This puts you at a distinct disadvantage and will result in you giving up more than you need to cement the relationship. You may as well have a 'kick me' sign on your back!

If at some point during the negotiation you determine that the relationship is unlikely to end up a win–win situation, then it is time to thank your counterpart and graciously walk away. This is an infinitely more positive outcome than creating a bad relationship. Sponsorship is notoriously incestuous—if you burn a bridge, it will come back to haunt you.

Payment arrangements

Sometimes the payment arrangements will be as important to a sponsor as the amount of money committed, so you need to be prepared to work with them.

Spreading payments across time

Oftentimes, a sponsor will want to spread payments over time. There are several reasons for this but the two overriding reasons are:

1. Comfort level—they want some assurance that the event is actually going ahead and that the benefits promised are being delivered. Often, once you have gone through the first year of a sponsorship, the sponsor will be more comfortable paying the entire fee up front.
2. Budgeting—if they have already budgeted for that time period, they may need to access quarterly marketing funds or some other kind of time-bound budgets.

Whatever the reason, you need to be prepared to work with the sponsor. You should endeavour to secure a substantial proportion of the fee up-front, both as a measure of good faith and to assist you in your cash flow in the lead up to your event.

It is reasonable that fees above a given amount ($15 000–$20 000) be paid in instalments. One common way of doing this is to request one-third upon signing of the agreement, another third three months later, and the final instalment two weeks before the event starts.

Ongoing contracts, such as sponsorships of cultural organisations or sporting teams, may be paid annually, semi-annually or quarterly.

Also keep in mind that if you are negotiating a small sponsorship with a company that has a major sponsorship budget, it may be more convenient for them to pay the entire amount at once. The only way to know which payment option they prefer is to ask.

Spreading payments across budgeting cycles

It may be necessary to spread payments across financial years, particularly for larger sponsorships or investments made after the current period has been budgeted. This can often make finding the money for your opportunity easier for the sponsor.

Companies' financial years vary widely, with multinationals often mirroring the financial year in their home country. Some companies have their own fiscal year. You should have found out what financial year they operate under during your initial research but, as a general guideline, here are a few typical periods:

➤ United States: 1 January–31 December

➤ Japan: 1 April–31 March

➤ Australia/New Zealand: 1 July–30 June

➤ United Kingdom: 1 April–31 March.

Multi-year agreements

When structuring a multi-year agreement, keep in mind the following things:

➤ If your event is new and will likely grow more valuable as time goes on, you should structure your fees to reflect larger payments in later years.

➤ If your event has a long track record of delivering the goods, you may elect a flat payment structure.

➤ If your event is new and you have one key sponsor who is the 'perceived owner' of the event, you *may* be able to get a larger fee in the first year to assist in underwriting the infrastructure but this will come at a dramatic cost in future years.

Proactively offer incentive-based fees

We are strongly in favour of fee structures that incorporate a component that is performance-based. This creates an incentive for the sponsee to deliver as promised—to go that extra mile—and sponsors see this as a refreshing departure from sponsees that take the money and run.

It also means that you could make more money on the sponsorship because you are lowering the risk to the sponsor (and let's face it, sponsors still tend to think sponsorship is a risk!). The key is to tie the performance-based component to specific, quantifiable and desirable outcomes.

Instead of charging $10 000 cash for a sponsorship, you could do this:

➤ $8000 up-front payment

➤ $2000 if exit polls reveal over 60 per cent unprompted awareness for the sponsorship

➤ $2000 if over 2000 people participate in database-generating activities.

This gives you a total of $12 000, reduces the perceived risk to the sponsor and shows that you are absolutely confident that you will produce results. Of course, if you are not confident of producing results, do not do it. In fact, if you are not confident of producing results, get out of sponsorship!

Special note on sales-based incentives

When incentive-based fees are mentioned to sponsors, they will often immediately want to negotiate an incentive based upon sales. Whatever you do, don't agree to a sales-based incentive.

You can provide a lot of the ingredients to making a sale, including:

➤ promoting the product

Incentive-based fees lower the perceived risk to the sponsor.

Never agree to a sales-based fee.

➤ enhancing the product's image

➤ providing opportunities for sales (e.g. on-site sales or sales to your members)

➤ product demonstrations

➤ relationship-building opportunities.

What you can't deliver are actual sales, as these will be largely based upon the quality and value inherent in the product. For instance, a soft drink manufacturer may be the exclusive vendor at your summer event but if a malfunction occurs and the drinks are warm and flat, or if they price it above market value, they won't hit sales projections no matter how many people you get through your gate. You should not be held accountable for that.

It is far better to negotiate an incentive based upon how many people come to your event and leave delivering the right product at the right price to your sponsor.

Contra sponsorship

Contra sponsorship occurs when a sponsor pays for their sponsorship with products or services instead of cash. Also known as barter, trade or in-kind sponsorship, contra sponsorship makes up at least a portion of a large number of sponsorships.

When negotiating for contra sponsorship, keep three things in mind.

1. Contra sponsorship is only of value to you if:
    (a) you have budgeted for the specific item already. In that case it is only worth as much as it is saving you in cash expenditure. For example, if a company offers to loan you $10 000 in new computer equipment when your planned expenditure was only $2000 lease payments, the offer is only worth $2000 to you.
    (b) it adds value to your other sponsorship packages. For instance, if you secure an airline sponsor, you could include air tickets to your event with your other sponsorship packages, making them more attractive for other potential sponsors.
2. If the contra sponsor is saving you cash, they are as valuable to you as a fully cash sponsor and they need to be serviced as a cash sponsor (see Part 3).
3. You still need money to run your event or property, so endeavour to negotiate sponsorships where contra sponsorship is only a component of the investment.

There's more to contra sponsorship than you think

When they hear the word 'contra', most people think only of a sponsored product—an airline providing free travel, a high-technology company providing computers, and so on.

> Contra sponsorship is only of value if you have budgeted for that item already.

The fact is that sponsors have access to dozens of opportunities and services that can save you a lot of money. What follows is a generic sponsor contra list. This is a great tool to use when negotiating with a sponsor, particularly one that is baulking at making the full investment in cash.

Promotion

➤ Media promotion

➤ Promotion of sponsee through retailers

➤ Promotion of sponsee on-pack

➤ Promotion in internal employee communication

➤ Promotion to customers (mailings, magazine, newsletter, Web site, database, etc.)

➤ Sponsee signage on sponsor building

Media

➤ Access to heavily discounted media rates through sponsor's media buyer

➤ Tags on existing advertising

➤ New advertisements profiling sponsee

➤ Providing a limited media schedule (probably shared with sponsor)

Creativity

➤ Creative work for the sponsee done by sponsor's advertising agency or in-house graphic department

People

➤ Provision of sponsor-contracted celebrity for event endorsement or appearances

➤ Donation of employee for fixed term assignment (full- or part-time for set number of weeks/months)

➤ Employee volunteers to augment on-site staff

➤ Access to in-house experts and subcontractors (public relations, printing, media planning, database development, etc.)

Infrastructure

➤ Office space

➤ Office equipment or services

➤ Event equipment or services

Other contra products or services

➤ For use as prizes, incentives or giveaways

➤ To add value to other sponsorship packages

Travel

➤ Access to discounted airline or hotel deals

➤ Contra travel or hotel (if sponsor is in travel business)

Contracts

When entering into a sponsorship agreement, the hope is always that the sponsorship will go perfectly and the terms of the contract will never be called into play. Unfortunately, this is not always the case, so it is important to understand the issues.

Types of agreements

Always have some sort of written agreement in force. The more formal the agreement, the more likely it will be complete and legally binding. In order of desirability, these are the types of agreements you could have:

1. a legal contract drawn up by a lawyer and bearing signatures and company seals of both organisations

2. a legal contract adapted from a template drawn up by a lawyer (we have included a comprehensive pro forma which has been created for this book by Allen Allen & Hemsley, Australia), bearing signatures and company seals of both organisations

3. a legal contract adapted from a template drawn up by a lawyer, bearing signatures of both organisations

4. a letter of agreement outlining all points of agreement, including benefits, communication and payment dates, and signed by both organisations

5. a confirmation letter from the sponsee outlining the benefits and payment dates (this is not desirable and should be avoided).

Determine at what level you need a letter of agreement or a contract. Often a letter of agreement, signed by both parties, will be used for sponsorships valued at under a certain amount, anywhere from $5000 to $20 000. Above that amount, a full contract will be required.

If you have a good **Sponsorship Agreement Pro Forma** (see page 185), it will make your job much easier when it comes to developing an appropriate agreement.

This is a very useful tool that can be utilised in several ways:

➤ as the basis for your agreement

➤ as your 'first pass' at a legal contract which will then be given to a lawyer for fine tuning (saving you a considerable amount in legal fees)

➤ as a reference, so that you are aware of possible issues and legal considerations.

We do not recommend using the pro forma as the basis for your agreement unless you have a lawyer check the agreement prior to entering into it.

Who should provide the contract

It is nearly always quicker and more straightforward for the sponsee to develop the contract, as corporate legal departments are notoriously bureaucratic and often develop contracts that are difficult to read and less than win–win.

Resolving disputes

When structuring an agreement, always try to work in a series of steps for resolving any conflicts that might arise. You only move onto the next step when what you have already tried has not worked. The four basic steps are, in order:

1. **Discussion**—This means having a meeting with the express purpose of coming to a resolution that is agreeable to both parties.

2. **Mediation**—This involves getting an independent arbiter to mediate a discussion between the parties, ensuring that they stay on track and open to solutions.

3. **Arbitration**—This is similar to mediation, except that the parties agree that the arbiter will hear both sides and make a decision. Beware, this could be almost as expensive as litigation.

4. **Litigation**—A long and usually expensive foray into the legal system to be avoided if at all possible.

Exclusivity

The only rule of exclusivity is: the more exclusivity is granted, the more valuable it is.

There are three types of exclusivity:

1. sponsorship

2. signage (in cases where the venue may have existing conflicting signage)

3. sales.

You can grant exclusivity across any or all of these areas.

Most exclusivity is granted on the basis of categories and is often referred to in contracts as 'category exclusivity'. This usually refers to the category of business that a company is in, for example, airline, carbonated soft drink, ice-cream or beer. You can make this exclusivity more valuable and attractive to your sponsor by extending it across competitive categories.

An example of this would be to grant Pepsi sponsorship and sales exclusivity across categories such as: carbonated soft drink (their true category), non-carbonated soft drinks, sports drinks, fruit juices, fruit and iced-tea based drinks, flavoured milk and water.

Exclusive sales provisions could contravene trade practices or anti-trust laws. This is another reason why it is important for a lawyer to prepare or check your agreement.

Sponsorship agreement pro forma

Included in the Appendix is a **Sponsorship Agreement Pro Forma** that was developed specifically for us by Lionel Hogg, Partner of Allen Allen & Hemsley. The full agreement can also be found on disk.

This sample agreement may be a useful starting point for a sponsorship agreement. However, it is very general because it is impossible to draft a document that accounts for all situations or for legal differences in all countries.

Ideally, it should be used as a template that is completed by the sponsee and sponsor and then given to a lawyer to check the drafting, change it to suit the law of the relevant place and better outline the rights of the parties. This will ensure that the agreement process is collaborative and will probably cost you far less than securing a lawyer to draft an agreement from scratch.

Warning

This document is provided as a sample only and is not a substitute for legal advice. You should seek the advice of a suitably qualified and experienced lawyer before using this document.

In particular, you or your lawyer should:

➤ check the law in your jurisdiction—make sure this agreement works there

➤ check for changes to the law—law and practice might have altered since this document was drafted or you last checked the situation

➤ modify wherever necessary—review this document critically and never use it without first amending it to suit your needs as every sponsorship is different

➤ beware of limits of expertise. If you are not legally qualified or are not familiar with this area of the law, do not use this document without first obtaining legal advice about it.

How this Agreement works

The Agreement assumes that there are standard clauses that should be in every Agreement and special clauses needed for your sponsorship. The standard clauses that should apply all of the time are called the 'Standard Conditions'. The parts that relate to your specific sponsorship are the 'Schedules' and the 'Special Conditions'.

The Schedules and the Special Conditions have precedence over the Standard Conditions. In other words, what you insert is more important than what is already written. This is why it is vital to use a lawyer or know about what you are doing.

Read the Agreement

Before doing anything, read the Agreement and see how it might apply to your situation. There might be Standard Conditions that are unsuitable. There might be new conditions you need to add. Do not assume that the Agreement is right for you.

The sample agreement is for an *exclusive* sponsorship for the relevant sponsorship category.

Complete the Schedules

You should complete each Schedule following the guidance notes in that Schedule.

For example, Schedule 23 is called 'Sponsor's termination events'. The guidance note tells you to see clause 9.2. You should read clause 9.2 and understand the circumstances in which the sponsor has a right to terminate the agreement. You should then insert in Schedule 23 any other circumstances peculiar to your sponsorship (e.g. the sponsor might want to terminate the agreement if the team being sponsored loses its licence to play in the major league or if the contracted lead performers for the musical withdraw their services).

Add Special Conditions

The Special Conditions (at the end of the Schedules) enable you to insert other conditions that are not dealt with by this sample agreement.

Changing Standard Conditions

You should *not* change the Standard Conditions without consulting a lawyer. The Agreement is drafted as a package and changing the Standard Conditions might have an unintended, domino effect on other terms.

If you have to change the Standard Conditions, do so by adding a Special Condition, such as, 'clause 18 of the Standard Conditions does not apply'.

Sign the Agreement

The parties sign and date the document on the last page. Make sure that the person with whom you do the deal is authorised to sign.

Finding a lawyer

You should consult a lawyer practising in your jurisdiction and experienced in sponsorship matters. If you don't have a good sponsorship lawyer, there are a number of sports law organisations around the world that can provide a referral, or you can contact Allen Allen & Hemsley in Australia.

Although you may not be a sporting organisation, these associations will be a great source for referrals, as sponsorship law skills are quite transferable across sponsorship genres.

Full contact details for a number of these organisations can be found in the Appendix.

If you have questions about the pro forma agreement

If you or your lawyer have questions about the **Sponsorship Agreement Pro Forma,** you are welcome to contact its author:

Lionel Hogg, Partner

Allen Allen & Hemsley

PO Box 7082 Riverside Centre

Brisbane Qld 4001 Australia

Phone: (61-7) 3334 3170

Fax: (61-7) 3334 3444

e-mail: lionel.hogg@aahq.com.au

Part 3

servicing

Chapter 9

Sponsorship planning and management

Sourcing and acquiring new sponsors is not the hardest part of a sponsorship manager's job. Servicing your sponsor is when the real work begins. Sponsorship is all about building and maintaining long-term relationships. The primary responsibility of organisations receiving sponsorship is to build positive relationships with their sponsors by ensuring that all agreed benefits are provided within the negotiated time frame.

It is equally important that organisations are committed to ensuring that their sponsors are provided with information, feedback and quantitative and qualitative research results that will assist their sponsors in determining if their objectives have been met. Simply providing the sponsor with the contracted benefits and a media report at the end of the event means you are only doing half the job.

Sponsors require and deserve total commitment from their sponsees. Evaluation is perhaps one of the most overlooked areas of sponsorship servicing today. The most successful sponsorship managers provide complete sponsorship service, which includes in-depth ongoing summary evaluation and assessment.

There is no secret on how to manage your sponsorships effectively. Once you have acquired your sponsorship, it comes down to three simple steps:

1. **develop** a sponsorship plan
2. **implement** the sponsorship plan
3. **evaluate** the sponsorship plan.

Develop the sponsorship plan

Once you have found a sponsor for your event you must firstly develop a sponsorship plan. The sponsorship plan defines what you and the sponsee want to achieve and how you are going to manage the sponsorship. Each sponsorship, regardless of its size or value, requires its own plan.

Every sponsorship plan should include:

➤ an executive summary

➤ a situation analysis

➤ a list of objectives

➤ strategies to meet those objectives

➤ performance indicators that will be used to measure the success of those strategies

➤ target audiences

➤ an action list/timeline/accountability list

➤ a budget

➤ an evaluation strategy.

A sponsorship plan states what you want to achieve, how you are going to achieve it and how you will know when you have achieved it. A **Sponsorship Implementation Plan Template** can be found on page 136.

In terms of quantifying returns on a sponsorship investment, a sponsorship plan provides you with two critical strategies for measuring returns—performance indicators and evaluation. If it is in your plan, you will not forget it. You will also have agreement from within your organisation and from the sponsor as to what you are trying to achieve and how you will measure the results.

Implement the sponsorship plan

Sponsorship is about creating an effective relationship between your organisation and the sponsor. Managing the sponsorship or implementing a well-thought-out sponsorship plan is about building and maintaining that relationship.

Evaluating the sponsorship plan

If you have followed your sponsorship plan, you will have identified performance indicators and ways of measuring or evaluating whether the sponsor has successfully met their sponsorship objectives. The best sponsorship implementation and evaluation plans are drawn up in consultation with your sponsors.

Your evaluation plan should include the following, some of which you will provide and some the sponsor will carry out:

> Each sponsorship, regardless of its size, requires a sponsorship plan.

> pre- and post-sponsorship surveys
> sales or visitation figures at your event
> qualitative research results
> media assessment.

Sponsorship implementation plan

Service1.doc

You should create a sponsorship implementation plan for each of your sponsors. This should be comprehensive, providing a blueprint for the execution of the program.

Introduction

Include details on the overall aims and objectives of the sponsorship plan. Briefly outline the strategies that you will undertake to assist the sponsor in meeting the objectives.

Situational analysis

Give a brief overview of where the sponsorship is at, who the key contacts are and any major issues that might affect the sponsorship.

If the sponsorship is ongoing, outline the past history of the sponsorship, recommendations and tactics that will be undertaken to refocus the sponsorship.

Sponsorship objectives

In dot points, detail the objectives of the sponsorship. Remember, objectives must always be SMART—specific, measurable, achievable, results-oriented and time-bound.

Each objective should be followed by a list of quantification mechanisms relevant to the objective. For example, one of the sponsor's objectives is to create a contact database of five thousand exhibition attendees intending to purchase a luxury car within the next twelve months, and they want to achieve that by the fourth week. Your quantification mechanisms may be:

> number of names on the database
> quality of information on the database
> timeliness of capturing the information
> timeliness of forwarding the completed database to the sponsor.

Determine quantification mechanisms with your sponsor as you work with them to develop your sponsorship objectives.

Target markets

Who are the target markets? Who else might this program affect? Your list may include staff, audiences, senior management, media and ticket holders.

Sponsorship benefits

Include a list of all benefits that have been included in the sponsorship contract as well as a list of any other benefits that may have been agreed to. A detailed list will assist both the sponsors and the sponsee in keeping tabs on the marketing opportunities available.

Evaluation

You should work with your sponsor to determine how they will measure the success of the sponsorship program. Detail how the sponsorship will be evaluated through key performance indicators.

Action list

Detail every marketing activity, event, media launch, report, meeting and every aspect of the provision of benefits and information you have promised the sponsor. Next to the item, indicate the time frame and person responsible.

Budget

Detail all costs that are required to make this sponsorship plan happen. Ensure you have accurately costed support and management of the sponsorship. Use your organisation's formula for calculating real staff and administration costs of employment (including overheads). See 'Calculating overheads' on page 44 for more information.

| Objective-based quantification

In the past, sponsors and sponsees have often tried to put dollar figures on the value of everything delivered and then crossed their fingers that this figure came up to something more than what was paid. If their estimates fell short, the sponsorship manager would often whack some arbitrarily large dollar amount on the bottom and call it 'good corporate citizenship'. There is no question that many sponsorship managers have covered their behinds with that old gem.

Double check your costs

When calculating costs, be sure to look at every benefit promised and every objective to be met. These costs will vary widely depending upon the type of event and benefits offered. Listed below are some of the more common costs encountered to get you started:

- VIP hospitality—tickets, invitations, catering, parking, gifts, security, travel/transport and accommodation
- signage—production, maintenance, construction, storage, backdrops, transport
- advertising—design, production, media time/space, agency advice
- endorsement or appearance fees
- promotional material—design, printing, shipping
- prize money, competition prizes
- product samples and discounts
- legal fees
- media/public relations support— media kits (design and production), media training, photographers, launch venue
- evaluation—research fees, media monitoring, compilation of data
- servicing costs—staff costs (remember to calculate the real cost of employment), consultants, travel.

> Quantifying sponsorship in terms of dollars doesn't work.

What good sponsorship practitioners have come to realise is that, although there are some objectives that can be quantified in dollars, such as sales, it is impossible to put an accurate dollar figure on many very important aspects of sponsorship, including the:

➤ association with sponsee attributes (image transfer)

➤ publicity

➤ signage

➤ television coverage

➤ awareness of sponsorship

➤ shifts in consumer perception of the sponsor.

Objective-based quantification is the most recent and useful trend for quantification since sponsorship began. It brings the results of sponsorship right back to what the sponsor is trying to achieve in their marketing program.

The other argument against quantifying sponsorship in terms of dollars is that this creates an unnatural preoccupation on the sponsor's part with 'getting their money's worth'. If we equate this with above-the-line advertising, it would be like a sponsorship manager patting him or herself on the back and calling it a day because s/he paid $200 000 and got $220 000 worth of television advertising. Whether the advertisements actually achieved anything has not been quantified at all. It is exactly the same with quantifying sponsorship. Whichever way you look at it, if you are quantifying an entire sponsorship program in terms of dollars, you are quantifying the process, not the results, and that's just plain silly.

Making the sponsor's investment quantifiable

Quantification is another one of those areas that is primarily the sponsor's responsibility but with which you should be involved from the outset. And if your sponsor is not thinking in terms of quantification at all, you may need to do some gentle education. In any case, if you can assist the sponsor to see the full value of their investment in terms of objective-based outcomes, you will already have made your case for renewal of sponsorship.

Before developing quantification mechanisms, you must keep in mind the following rules:

➤ Benchmarking is a must. You can't know what you have achieved if you don't know where you started.

➤ Specify quantification mechanisms from the outset.

➤ Don't try to change everything into a dollar value because it really doesn't work.

The basis of this type of quantification is that it's all about objectives and, if objectives are SMART, they should be quantifiable.

Each objective should be made as clear and specific as possible. Generalisations and ambiguity virtually guarantee that a sponsorship will be unquantifiable. Even if your organisation has given a stellar performance on the sponsorship, it will be impossible to prove that you have delivered on the objectives. And we hate to break it to you but, as a sponsorship seeker, the assumption by sponsors (and particularly their Boards) is that if you can't prove it, you haven't done it.

More importantly to you, if you don't know exactly what the sponsor is trying to achieve, you will not be able to deliver it.

We often see sponsors specify their objectives in a series of two-word phrases, such as 'increase sales'. While this is certainly a worthwhile pursuit, neither you nor the sponsor will be able to determine the extent to which this objective has been met because it is too vague. When faced with vague objectives such as this, you need to keep asking questions until you have agreed upon a SMART objective.

For example, if you have developed an initial objective of 'increasing sales', you could ask the following types of questions:

➤ What type of sales (new customer, incremental, loyalty or up-selling)?
➤ Through what distribution channel (retail, catalogue, hotline, etc.)?
➤ To which target market(s)?
➤ During what time frame?
➤ From what benchmark?
➤ Determined how?

The table below provides some examples of typical short, snappy (but non-quantifiable) objectives and how they might be turned into SMART objectives.

> Beware of two-word objectives.

NOT	INSTEAD
Increase sales	Create incremental sales of 10 per cent over the benchmark of $240 000 per week during the six-week promotional period, as determined by retailer case commitments.
Develop database	Develop a database of no less than 2500 qualified prospects, as determined by salary level, age range, professional and family status, and current insurance products owned. A profile of acceptable ranges is attached.
Gain publicity	Gain a minimum of ten high-level and fifteen medium-level publicity placements, as determined by the agreed Media Evaluation Model, over the six-week promotional period. An overview of the target market indicators and marketing messages is attached.

(Cont.)

What are all those kind of sales?

Just like there are different kinds of customers, there are also different kinds of sales. To demonstrate the difference between the four main types of sales, let's think about them in terms of a fast-food chain:

- New customer. Someone who has never been to the fast-food chain comes in for the first time.
- Loyalty. An existing customer starts coming in for lunch more often or starts coming in for other meals as well.
- Incremental sales. 'Do you want fries with that?' In other words, when someone buys more items of food than they were planning (or than they usually do) on any given visit.
- Up-selling. 'For just 50 cents you can upgrade to a Great Big Meal.' In other words, buying an item that is bigger or more expensive than originally planned.

NOT	INSTEAD
Demonstrate 'good corporate citizenship'	Increase public opinion on our company's professionalism (from 45 per cent positive to 64 per cent), commitment to Australia (from 12 per cent to 35 per cent) and propensity to buy (from 22 per cent to 36 per cent) over the six-month promotional period, as determined by responses to our annual public opinion survey. A profile of the target markets is attached.

After looking at the examples in the above table you may be thinking to yourself, 'these objectives are so specific, they can't possibly encompass the entire value of the sponsorship'. You're right, there are a number of areas that are very difficult to quantify directly. What you should try to do is to develop with your sponsor not one but several SMART objectives that will quantify key aspects of the sponsorship and be indicative of the overall success of their investment.

Once the objectives have been fully developed, the big question for the sponsor is 'If these objectives are achieved, will you consider this sponsorship to have been a success?'. If the answer is no, then the objectives need to be developed or extended further. If the answer is yes, you know exactly what you are working towards.

Quantification mechanisms

The most vexing part of creating SMART objectives is the 'M' part, that is, making them measurable. Do not despair, however, as there are many more ways to measure sponsorship results than you realise.

Depending upon what objectives the sponsor is trying to achieve, you can work with them to ensure that one or more mechanisms are in place for each objective. Some suggestions on quantification mechanisms for different categories of objectives can be found below.

Sales—new customer, incremental, up-selling or loyalty sales

- Retail figures
- Scanner data
- Case commitments
- Sales promotion participation
- On-site or direct sales (sales at or as a direct result of your event)
- Coupon redemptions
- Profit margins

Customer or general public perceptions/behaviour

➤ Quantitative research (against benchmark)

➤ Qualitative research (against benchmark)

Database/loyalty marketing

➤ Number and quality of people joining the database

➤ Loyalty activity

➤ Sales or media promotion participation

➤ Merchandising (members/customers buying brand event merchandise through your sponsor)

Media promotion

➤ Number and quality of media placements (see the **Media Evaluation Model** on page 143)

➤ Media exposure of marketing message

➤ Media exposure of logo

Product/attribute awareness

➤ Entrance/exit awareness surveys

➤ Target market awareness surveys

➤ General public awareness surveys

Employees

➤ Product knowledge contest results

➤ Incentive program results

➤ Awareness and attitude surveys

➤ Merchandise program sales

Key customers

➤ Incentive program results—long- and short-term

➤ Relationship-building opportunities

Retailers

➤ Number and quality of retail displays

➤ Number of newspaper specials

➤ Preference/attitude surveys

➤ Relationship-building opportunities

Quantifying media

If you have ever been guilty of handing a sponsor a stack of media clippings at the end of an event, whether they have anything to do with the sponsorship or not (and most of us have at one time or another!), now is the time to clean up your act.

That approach to quantifying media is called media monitoring—literally providing copies of all media clippings, television and radio interview transcripts and tapes without any analysis of their value. Unfortunately, a folder of articles and clippings provides the sponsor with few tangible results. Your media monitoring activities will be greatly enhanced if you provide your sponsors with a media assessment report.

Media assessment report

There is no question that it is difficult to assess the monetary value of a newspaper article or a television interview. There are a number of methods available but results of these evaluation methods vary widely. Instead of trying to quantify a highly nebulous aspect of sponsorship in terms of hard and fast dollars, we strongly advocate a more objective-oriented approach. Not only does this bring media evaluation into line with the quantification of the entire sponsorship but it also removes all question as to what the sponsor is trying to achieve through media coverage.

In preparing your sponsorship plan and evaluation strategies, work with the corporate sponsorship manager to determine the specific kinds of results they are seeking. How do they evaluate their media placements? By working closely with the sponsorship manager, you will ensure that both organisations understand how you will evaluate the media gained and what specific results you are seeking.

A media assessment report might include the following:

➤ determination of the quality of exposure

➤ audience demographic details

➤ type of coverage

➤ key messages communicated

➤ prominence and position

➤ theme of articles and interviews

➤ reach of media—geographic, size of audience, range of media

➤ sponsorship acknowledgment by number of articles and interviews.

We have provided a very simple **Media Evaluation Model** that will assist you in evaluating each media placement in terms of the key indicators: the marketing message communicated and the target market reached. If you or your sponsor do not have a strong, objective-based media quantification mechanism in place, this may work very well for you.

Media evaluation model

There are literally dozens of ways to evaluate the results of your sponsorship-driven publicity campaign. What we have come up with is a **Media Evaluation Model** that brings unpaid media coverage straight back to objectives. Each piece of media coverage is rated based on the two major criteria for sponsorship success:

1. the success in communicating the sponsor's marketing message(s)
2. the success in reaching the target market(s).

This means that you must know specifically what the sponsor is trying to communicate and who exactly they are trying to reach with this message. Discuss this up-front with the sponsor. Don't guess.

Marketing message

Each portion of the marketing message is rated on a scale of 0–10. The levels at which each score is reached must be determined and agreed with the sponsor prior to commencing the sponsorship. Some suggestions are:

➤ 0 = no mention of the sponsor whatsoever (it doesn't matter *how* good the coverage of the sponsee)

➤ 4 = maximum number allocated to logo exposure or simple sponsor mention (it will usually be lower)

➤ 6 = minimum number allocated to communication of the sponsor's marketing message.

Target markets

Target market evaluations will be based upon the portion of the defined target marketplace that is reached with that communication. Keep in mind that if an article, for instance, appears in a publication that reaches only five thousand people, but that they represent 80 per cent of your target audience, that is more valuable than an article appearing in a mass market newspaper that reaches only 15 per cent of your marketplace.

Given this, we suggest that one way of determining a score for target markets will be to give 1–2 points for each 10 per cent of your total target market reached.

Plotting the results

When you multiply the scores for each result, anything that scores under 16 total should be considered to be of little or no value to the sponsor. Anything that scores between 16 and 36 is of medium value. And anything that scores above 36 should be considered to be of high value to the sponsor.

This can be graphically represented on a chart, which will look something like the one shown in the following figure.

Figure 9.1

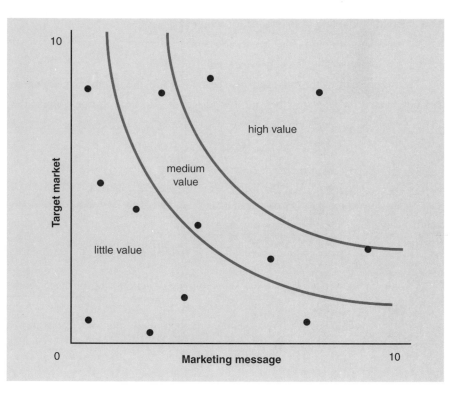

So...what's a 100?

Let's say that a dairy corporation supplying milk to one major city sponsors a football team. The marketing message is 'Milk for health and fitness'. They target a wide variety of people with their various milk products but are geographically limited to the one city. Imagine after a particularly great game, the local daily newspaper has a front-page photograph of a great tackle with the logo showing clearly and the headline, 'They must be drinking their milk'. That placement would score 10 on each, for a total of 100—an outstanding result!

Managing the sponsor

Although sponsors are generally becoming much more professional in the way that they do business, as a major stakeholder you will probably still find yourself managing the process at one time or another. The following information should help.

Sponsee information kit

In your first meeting with the sponsor once the contract is signed, we suggest providing the sponsor with an information kit that contains the following items:

➤ details and an overview of responsibilities for all key contacts on your side

➤ a copy of your sponsorship plan

➤ media/marketing matrix, showing dates for all marketing activities, preferably including the promotional activities of all sponsors as well

➤ key dates and deadlines

➤ artwork, including any guidelines, PMS colours etc., both as bromides and on disk

➤ logo approval process (for sponsor using your logo)

➤ approval fax cover sheet (the idea is that whenever your staff see this cover sheet, you know that it requires review and approval within a specified approval period)

➤ any other information or materials that will streamline the sponsorship process.

Sponsor information kit

At that same meeting, we suggest you also request an information kit from your sponsor that contains the following items:

- details and an overview of responsibilities for all key contacts on the sponsor's side
- a restatement of their objectives for this sponsorship, your target markets, core brand values etc.
- how the sponsorship and sponsee performance will be evaluated (key performance indicators)
- a template for written reports created by the sponsor in the format they need
- artwork, including any guidelines, PMS colours and so on, both as bromides and on disk
- any other information or materials that will streamline the sponsorship process.

Regular meetings

No, having a beer with them in the sky box does not count. You need to hold regular meetings with the sponsor from inception of the contract right through to the conclusion. This will ensure that you are aware of their situation and goals at all times and will ensure you keep on top of all developments, opportunities and potential trouble spots.

As for timing, we find bi-weekly meetings to be very beneficial. Under no circumstances should you go longer than a month between meetings.

Written updates

If you only have time to meet monthly, then you should definitely be providing a mid-month written update to your sponsor. This only needs to be a concise report of where the sponsorship is, noting anything that is currently outstanding. Ask the sponsor from the outset what information they will need so there is no confusion.

Put everything in writing

It is important to put everything in writing. This way, you have some recourse if something does not get done, addressed or checked. Every time you meet, someone needs to take notes and confirm all action items, including responsibilities and timelines, in writing.

Also, if something needs doing between meetings (and it always does), be sure to put that in writing as well. It does not need to be formal, just a quick fax or e-mail will be sufficient.

Chapter 10

Maximisation

Maximisation, to a sponsor, means getting the greatest possible benefit from an investment of money, time or other resources. You may be thinking to yourself, 'What does this have to do with me?'. Although maximising a sponsorship is primarily the sponsor's responsibility, you are not completely off the hook.

Even as sponsorship has become more sophisticated, there are still companies who believe that simply becoming a sponsor will achieve their objectives so they don't need to support it. This type of investment is destined to under-perform. Understanding some of the options for maximising a sponsorship will allow you to educate your sponsor gently and encourage them to utilise their partnership with your organisation fully. We all know that a happy sponsor is a good sponsor, so helping them to achieve their goals is always in your best interest.

There is a rule of thumb that states that for every dollar a sponsor spends on a sponsorship fee, they need to spend another dollar to maximise the sponsorship. This rule is useful if you are working with a sponsor who really does not understand that the sponsorship must be supported, but can prove somewhat limiting as this amount can vary a lot. In reality, the amount of support that a sponsor will need to commit to maximise a sponsorship fully will range from around 50 per cent of the sponsorship fee to over 400 per cent.

You are probably also wondering what to do with that 10–15 per cent of the sponsorship fee that we have told you to hold aside for servicing the sponsor. Again, that money is not to be used for taking them to lunch or for providing benefits that you have already promised in your agreement. It is for providing additional benefits that will assist your sponsor in achieving their objectives—*maximising* their sponsorship.

> Although maximisation is not your responsibility, encouraging it is always in your best interests.

> Support will cost the sponsor from 50 to 400 per cent on top of the sponsorship fee.

Integration

The primary mechanism for any sponsor to maximise their investment is to ensure that it is integrated. Companies around the world are spending billions of dollars on sponsorship. Unfortunately many of those sponsorships are running as self-contained units, having little if anything to do with their greater marketing program or objectives. Without the support of a fully integrated program, they are certainly not performing as well as they could.

Sponsors often think that integration will cost a large amount of money. In fact, integration can ease the burden of additional costs by fully utilising all of the marketing vehicles that the sponsor is already paying for. They can drop their costs dramatically, making their whole sponsorship program more cost-effective and making it easier to say yes to your offer.

Helping your sponsor to integrate in two ways

Again, integration is not primarily your responsibility. In fact, you will probably shock your sponsor if you take a proactive stance in maximising their sponsorship. Don't let this unfortunate lack of precedent dispel you, however, because sponsors will generally be very happy that you are taking an interest in their success.

The two ideal times to discuss how the sponsorship will be integrated into the sponsor's marketing program are:

1. during your initial sponsor research, when you will ascertain how the sponsor *usually* supports a sponsorship

2. during the negotiation phase, when you will discuss the specifics of integrating this sponsorship.

Not only will this add value to their sponsorship of your organisation but also to their greater sponsorship program, showing your total dedication to achieving their goals.

Although there are several ways for a sponsor to integrate their sponsorship program, the two ways that are appropriate for you to encourage are: integrating their team and integrating their marketing media.

Integrating their team

Encouraging your sponsor to create a team of decision makers from across departments and outside resources is a great first step. If they hold regular meetings with this team, it will provide them with additional opportunities for maximising their sponsorships, as well as pointing out potential trouble spots.

Encourage the sponsor not to overwhelm the group with 'marketing people'. You want to create a multifaceted think tank. Ask them to consider including representatives from the following areas:

Integration can make it easier for a sponsor to say yes to your offer.

Approach integration early in your discussions.

- advertising agency
- corporate communications
- customer service
- distribution
- employee representation
- key retailers
- market research
- merchandising
- packaging/production
- product management
- public relations
- relationship/loyalty marketing
- sales
- sales development
- sales promotion
- sponsorship consultant.

As their sponsorship partner, you should also be involved in all meetings around the planning and implementation of your sponsorship.

If your sponsor seems reluctant to create and administer a team like this, our suggestion is to ask permission from your sponsor to hold a meeting at your premises for representatives of the above departments/subcontractors. Position it as a one-off brainstorming session, which will be followed after the event by a debriefing session. This makes it easy for the sponsor to say yes to this valuable activity and, in many cases, the sponsor will see the value and continue the meetings internally.

Integrating their marketing media

Sponsorship is probably the easiest marketing activity to integrate across marketing media and there is no question that the results are the most dramatic. One needs to look no further than Pepsi or Nike to see that sponsorship really lends itself to this type of activity. Their sponsorships of people and events appear on everything from television commercials to product packaging.

This type of integration maximises the sponsor's program by marrying the power of sponsorship to the myriad marketing vehicles that they already have in place. Although there are still costs associated with integration, the cost is generally lower than creating separate supporting programs from scratch.

Figure 10.1

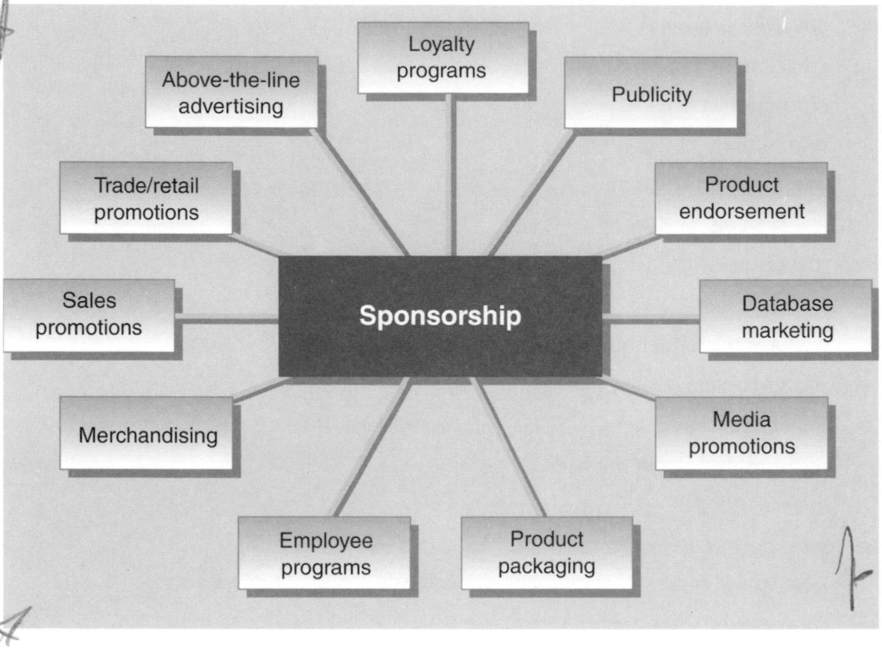

During the meeting with the sponsor's team, as outlined above, one of the primary questions should be, 'What are all the ways we can use this sponsorship across our existing marketing and communications programs?'. Some of the concepts will be great and some won't, but it takes a free flow of ideas in order to find the ones of value.

The good news for you as the sponsee is that every time the sponsor promotes the sponsorship through their various marketing channels, they are also promoting your event. Encouraging this type of integration can greatly extend your marketing reach and has real commercial value to your organisation.

> Integration has real commercial value to *your* organisation.

Maximisation options

There are dozens, if not hundreds, of ways to maximise a sponsorship. If you are going to assist your sponsor in achieving a fully maximised program, you should have at least a working knowledge of their options.

This section is also meant to give you an understanding of what the sponsor will go through in order to make their sponsorship of your organisation work. We are not suggesting that you do this for them but you should assist the sponsor in any way that you can. Don't fall into the trap of thinking that the sponsor has the easy job because making a sponsorship really deliver on objectives is hard work.

This is not an exhaustive study of the subject but outlines some of the more common ways of maximising a sponsorship.

Promotions

Promotion is the general term for a sponsor creating a sponsorship-driven activity in partnership with one or more other organisations that benefits all involved. These could include:

➤ media promotion

➤ sponsor cross-promotion

➤ non-sponsor cross-promotion

➤ retail promotion

➤ internal promotion.

The different types of promotions are defined below.

Media promotion

Media promotion is when a sponsor develops a cross-promotion with one or more media organisations. This is very common and can be extremely powerful—the more creative the execution the better.

EXAMPLE

A frozen pizza company is a sponsor of the local baseball team, along with a lot of other companies. They decide to stand out from the crowd by creating a promotion with one of the top radio stations in town, with winners attending spring training with the team in Florida, all expenses paid. The hook—contestants have to rewrite the words to the classic baseball anthem 'Take Me Out to the Ballgame', using the sponsor's name and pleading their case as to why they should be chosen. Entries, along with proofs of purchase of their pizzas, were sent to the radio station, with the best entries chosen to sing their songs on air. The result was terrific breakthrough and exceptionally strong linkages between the pizza company and the team.

Sponsor cross-promotion

This is when two or more sponsors work together to create a promotion that achieves objectives for each of them.

> You need to know what a sponsor goes through to maximise a sponsorship.

EXAMPLE

A surf clothing manufacturer and music retailer are both sponsors of a surf and skate festival. They are both targeting the same audience.

Using the event as the focal point of the promotion, they decide to work together to double the effectiveness of their support spend by structuring the following deal:

➤ *With every two CDs purchased from the music retailer, the customer receives a coupon redeemable for $10 off the purchase of two items of the sponsor's surf clothing. This creates a point of difference for the highly value-oriented customers of the music retailer, while driving people to retailers of surf clothing to redeem their coupons.*

➤ *With every $100 spent on the sponsor's surf clothing, the customer receives a voucher for a free CD from a selected range at the music sponsor's stores, offering a strong incentive for people to purchase that brand of surf clothing rather than any other brand carried by surf retailers. The surf clothing manufacturer then agreed to pay the music retailer a heavily discounted rate for each CD redeemed, and the music retailer further benefited because research has shown that most people buy more than one CD at a time.*

As sponsors of the same property, they already have something in common. They are also probably interested in the same marketplace (or at least segments of the same marketplace). It makes perfect sense that sponsors can get together to create cross-promotions that support both sponsorships—saving both parties money while doubling the communication base.

Some sponsees go to great lengths to keep their sponsors apart, afraid that they will compare notes on benefits and costs. We do not recommend this strategy and, instead, recommend that you facilitate sponsor co-operation. After all, if your sponsorships work better, you are more likely to have happy, productive sponsors that you will retain year after year.

> You should be proactive in getting your sponsors together.

Cross-promoting with non-sponsors

Sometimes it makes sense for sponsors to develop cross-promotions with companies outside of the circle of event sponsors.

EXAMPLE

A Web-based travel agency is a major sponsor of a large consumer travel expo. They are targeting the savvy vacation traveller with a new service set to revolutionise how computer users travel. As there is a necessary correlation between using the

service and having access to a computer, they decided to create a promotion with a non-sponsor computer manufacturer. The computer company was interested because there is a strong correlation between savvy vacation travellers and home computer owners and they also wanted an opportunity to showcase the exceptional multimedia and Internet capabilities of their machine.

At the event, the travel agency and computer company set up a large number of top-quality home computing machines, allowing the consumer to test drive both the service and the computer's capabilities. When a person logged on for a demonstration, they filled in a comprehensive, computer-based questionnaire, building a database and capturing information about both their travel habits and computer use. This also entered the consumer into a draw to win the vacation they requested using the service (further encouraging them to test the service to the fullest) and a home computer.

Cross-promoting with non-sponsors can provide a lot of freedom in selecting cross-promotional partners and, hence, excellent results can be gained. You must, however, be aware of some potential areas for conflict:

➤ Cross-promotions can be used by non-sponsors as a means for ambushing their competition. For example, if the event sponsor, Gatorade, created a promotion with non-sponsor Reebok, when Nike is among the other event sponsors. The deal may be great and their intentions may be honourable but you could be caught up in controversy. If you want to be seen as protecting your sponsors from ambush, you must ensure that no promotional partners are seen as competing, directly or indirectly, with your current sponsors.

➤ Even if there isn't a potential conflict involved, sponsees need to be careful about cross-promotions with non-sponsors. If you are not careful about limiting the benefits provided (through the sponsor) to their partner, you may end up with a situation where the non-sponsor is getting the benefits of sponsorship without paying a fee. Do two things: ensure your contract employs ample controls for passing on benefits to a partner; and be sure that the benefits delivered to your own organisation through the cross-promotion are greater than the perceived loss.

➤ Media can also be a problem. If an event has an official media and one of your sponsors does a media promotion with a competitor, there are likely to be some noses out of joint, although that rarely stops it from happening.

Warning: non-sponsor cross-promotions can be very problematic.

Retail cross-promotion

Retail cross-promotion involves the sponsor's retailers and/or distribution system and is often a key element in fully maximised sponsorship programs. Retail cross-promotion can add weight to other sales promotional activities and can serve to communicate the marketing message powerfully at the point of purchase.

EXAMPLE

A prestige car manufacturer took out the presenting sponsorship of a major national tour by a high-profile symphony orchestra. The car manufacturer was about to introduce a new roadster and decided to use the tour to launch the new car to their most influential customers.

The car manufacturer worked closely with their top dealers in each city to develop launch receptions for current owners of their marque. These receptions were held on opening night and featured the unveiling of the new car. Everything about the launch reeked of quality and prestige and, after the event, guests were treated to the opening night performance in the best seats in the house.

The dealers used the event to add value to their relationships with their top customers, underscoring not only the quality of the vehicles but the esteem in which the dealers hold their clients. To extend the relationship even further, after the event the dealer sent a thank you card to each client, along with a special-edition branded CD of the symphony orchestra.

Although the above example deals with a very targeted customer group, retail sponsorship can work just as well with a wide variety of retail outlets, such as grocery stores, specialty retailers or petrol stations.

On the side of the retailer, a powerful cross-promotion can serve to increase store traffic and sales, as well as to create a point of difference from the competition. In order to achieve this for the retailer, the sponsor must be willing to share perceived ownership of all or part of their sponsorship of your organisation.

As the sponsee, a major retail promotion driven by one of your sponsors can be an extraordinarily effective way to communicate your marketing message. So if it is not conflicting with other paying sponsors, we wholeheartedly recommend that you are proactive on this point.

Internal promotion

As powerful as sponsorship can be for communicating with a sponsor's customers, it can be just as powerful for communicating with their employees and shareholders. It can help them to increase their knowledge base, boost morale, increase productivity or simply give something back to the people who make their company what it is.

EXAMPLE

A large parcel delivery company realised that, although they had introduced a number of great new products, a lot of their employees did not understand the benefits or differences between them. So, they decided to use their long-standing relationship with that country's Olympic team to run an employee promotion developing product knowledge.

An Olympic-theme brochure was created, highlighting the main features of the whole range of products, accompanied by a small quiz on product features. This was distributed to all employees throughout the company, with correct responses entering a draw to attend the overseas Olympics as a representative of the company.

Simple as it may seem, this exercise increased employee product knowledge by over 50 per cent and, as part of a larger Olympic-driven employee program, worked very well to achieve specific staff objectives.

Within a larger sponsorship portfolio, it is not above the realm of possibility that a sponsor could select a sponsorship specifically to achieve employee-based objectives.

When looking at promoting sponsorships internally, be sure to think about what is important to the sponsor's employees. There are no hard and fast rules but here are some suggestions:

➤ merchandising, usually done to employees or shareholders at cost

➤ employee perks (merchandise, tickets, celebrity appearances, etc.)

> We strongly recommend retail cross-promotions.

> product knowledge programs
> incentive programs
> volunteer programs, creating fun ways for the sponsor's employees to become materially involved in the sponsorship
> contests for an employee to travel to a major event to be the company 'representative'
> 'family day at . . .' where employees and their families go for free.

Database generation and research

Many sponsors have a component of database marketing to their businesses. If they do any kind of mailings or billings, or have a loyalty program (e.g. frequent flyer points), they will probably be very interested in database development.

Even if actually generating a database is not a big priority, they may be very interested in using the sponsorship as a catalyst to poll their target market, gaining research on their opinions and purchasing habits. There are literally dozens of ways to generate database information around a sponsorship, including:

> ticket sales
> contests
> competitions
> toll-free numbers
> trial offers
> discount offers
> test drives
> coupons
> registrations
> point of sale material
> kids pages
> fan clubs
> Internet sites
> sales receipts
> information inquiries
> membership programs
> warranties
> welcome cards
> exit/entrance surveys

➤ post-event research
➤ product registration.

Once your sponsor has chosen one or more mechanisms for capturing data, they will need to decide what kind of information to ask. You need to keep it short and simple, but should capture:

➤ name
➤ address
➤ telephone number
➤ age
➤ occupation
➤ date and location of last purchase.

It can also be very useful to capture the following types of information, which serve the dual purpose of providing customer and potential customer research:

➤ income level
➤ what other brands they have tried
➤ their three most important product characteristics (e.g. quality, price, warranty, location of retailer, etc.)
➤ how often they purchase the product
➤ where they purchase the product (e.g. grocery store, petrol station, etc.)
➤ when they plan to make their next purchase of … (e.g. car, home loan, holiday, computer, etc.).

As you are reading through this, you should be thinking to yourself that these activities parallel nicely with the kind of research you want to be doing for your organisation or event. Working together with your sponsor can generate a lot of information very cost-effectively for both of you.

Database generation will often work well in concert with your event research.

Publicity

Publicity is often a cornerstone of sponsorship programs. There is plenty written about publicity and we are not pretending to be experts in this area but we offer the following general advice.

You can do several very simple things to help your sponsor maximise public relations around their investment:

➤ Work closely with your sponsor's public relations department or agency so that you are involved in any publicity activities they may undertake around the sponsorship.

➤ Include the sponsor's marketing message in all of your publicity activities and endeavour to weave that message into newsworthy angles.

➤ Ensure that your organisation's publicity activities include the sponsor's target marketplaces, even if they may not be your core markets (e.g. if your sponsor is an automobile manufacturer, ensure that the motoring press are included). Ask you sponsor who their specific targets are, including both consumer and intermediate customers.

Ambush protection

No other aspect of sponsorship has received as much attention in recent years as ambush marketing. Ambush marketing is, very simply, when a non-sponsor undertakes activities that do one or both of the following:

➤ Create confusion in the marketplace as to who the rightful sponsor is. This is often accomplished through the creation of promotions that have the look and feel of the event, or use similar or leading words, without actually saying they are a sponsor. The result is that the non-sponsor receives much of the benefit of being a sponsor without paying the fee.

➤ Undermine a rightful sponsor. Even if a company does not engage in the more obvious type of ambush outlined above, they can still cause problems for a rightful sponsor. A classic example is the major football event that was sponsored by a brewer. A rival brewer paid a stripper a few hundred dollars to streak across the field at an appropriate moment. The result was that virtually every newspaper in the country ran a photo of the streaker instead of the game on the front page of the sports section.

There are two ways for a sponsor to be protected against ambush, and even then it can happen.

Legal

The main problem with preventing ambush marketing is that most of the time it is perfectly legal. The only time that it is not legal is if the ambushing company falsely represents that they are a sponsor, claims endorsement by the sponsee, or blatantly mislead the public into believing these things to be true.

The best way to protect your sponsors through legal channels is to ensure that ambush protection is written into the contract. This will demonstrate that you will not under any circumstances sell sponsorship, vending rights or signage to any of the sponsor's competitors and will compel you to protect their rights within the scope of any media or subcontractor deals. But this is still only a partial measure because most ambushes have nothing directly to do with the sponsee.

Strategic

The best ambush protection a sponsor can possibly have is to maximise their sponsorship fully. If they have created a strong program of support for their investment, any activities mounted by their competition will look weak and stupid by comparison.

If you want to assist the sponsor in checking their vulnerability, work closely with them to assess potential risk areas and assist in any way you can to minimise those risks.

Conclusion

That's it . . . *The Sponsorship Seeker's Toolkit*. If your head is spinning and you're wondering if sponsorship is really worth all the effort, don't worry, that's normal. On the other hand, you may be so excited about the possibilities that you can't wait to put these systems into place in your organisation tomorrow. That's normal too. In fact, we wouldn't be surprised if you were feeling both ways!

There is no doubt that sponsorship is a sophisticated, demanding pursuit, and one that is easier to get wrong than right. Our aim in putting this book together is to provide you with a system for selling and servicing sponsorship, as well as the street smarts that will make operating in this complicated field miles easier.

We have developed and refined our approach over our combined twenty-seven years in sponsorship. The results enjoyed by the hundreds of participants in our workshops prove without a shadow of doubt that this approach works exceedingly well across a wide range of sponsorship seekers—from sport to culture to government, large organisations to small, beginners to seasoned professionals.

Asking for money is never easy. What we have provided you with are the theory and tools for creating successful partnerships. Our premise is simple and based on three key principles:

1. Ensure you fully understand your audience, values and attributes, and what you have to offer a sponsor.
2. Create a customised proposal that meets the marketing and business objectives of your potential sponsor.
3. Undersell and over-deliver.

There is no magic wand for sponsorship. Success revolves around good research and hard work. Consider the sales process as 75 per cent preparation, 10 per cent sales and 15 per cent follow-through, and you will be pretty close to the mark. Most organisations barely prepare, approach sales as a simple transaction, and don't follow up at all. It's no wonder that most sponsorship efforts fail.

No one can guarantee that every proposal you create will be successful. What we *can* guarantee you is that if you follow the Smart Marketing Streetwise Workshops system, your offers will have a much greater rate of success.

It is important that all of us as practitioners recognise that sponsorship marketing is a rapidly evolving marketing tool. We need to work together—sharing ideas, evaluation techniques and case studies—if we are to continue to succeed in creating win—win partnerships. Don't be afraid to share information, pricing and evaluation strategies and networks. Remember, what goes around comes around.

In the same vein, we would love to hear how this approach to sponsorship works for you and welcome your feedback. Our contact details can be found at the back of the book.

We have greatly enjoyed creating *The Sponsorship Seeker's Toolkit* for you and look forward to meeting many of you as we travel around the world doing workshops.

Wishing you successful sponsorships!

Anne-Marie and Kim

Part 4

appendix

Glossary

Above-the-line advertising
Traditional advertising venues—television, radio, newspaper, magazine and outdoor advertising. Also known as 'main media'.

Added value
The provision of an unexpected benefit to a customer or sponsor, primarily done to strengthen the relationship with them.

Advertising
Placing a commercial message in above-the-line media.

Advertorial
When a company purchases the right to place favourable editorial material or editorial material with a distinctly commercial slant in a publication or on a program for a fee. Generally, it must carry wording that clearly states that it is a paid advertisement.

Agent
An individual or organisation that sells sponsorship properties on a commission or fee basis. Also known as a 'broker'.

Ambush marketing
An organisation creating the perception that they are a sponsor of a property when they have not purchased the rights to that property.

Below-the-line advertising
Non-traditional advertising avenues (anything that is not 'above-the-line'), such as sponsorship, publicity, sales promotion, relationship or loyalty marketing, coupons, database marketing, direct response and retail promotions.

Broker
An individual or organisation that sells sponsorship properties on a commission or fee basis. Also known as an 'agent'.

Clutter
A term used to describe an overload of sponsor messages around one event. It is also used more generally to describe the massive amount of advertising and other marketing messages ever present in developed society today.

Contra
Term to describe products or services that are provided in lieu of cash in exchange for sponsorship rights. Also known as 'in-kind'.

Coverage
Media term referring to the proportion of the target market that has the opportunity to see or hear any one advertisement. It is

expressed as a percentage of the total target market. Also known as 'reach'.

Critical success factor

This refers to something you or your sponsor must do right for the sponsorship or event to be a success. Often there are a number of critical success factors for any given activity.

Cross-promotion

When two or more organisations create promotional opportunities that benefit all partners.

Donation

An offering of product or cash that is given by a company without any anticipated commercial return.

Exclusivity

Exclusive rights to sponsorship or on-site sales. Typically defined by the sponsor's category of business (e.g. 'exclusive automobile sponsor' or 'exclusive beer vendor').

Frequency

Media term referring to the average number of times each member of your target audience receives an advertising message over the course of the advertising campaign.

Grant

The provision of funds or material for a specific project generally not linked to a company's core business. The grant must usually be acknowledged by the recipient and generally must be acquitted. A grant is given on the basis of the need for the project rather than the promotional and marketing opportunities it may provide.

Image transfer

The process by which a sponsor associates itself with the core values and attributes of a sponsee, with the goal being to introduce or reinforce those attributes within their company or product.

In-kind

Term to describe products or services that are provided in lieu of cash in exchange for sponsorship rights. Also known as 'contra'.

In-pack

The promotion of a sponsorship in the sponsor's actual product packaging. Often done in conjunction with 'on-pack' promotion.

Launch

A public unveiling or announcement of the details of an event, program or sponsorship, which is specifically designed to gain publicity. The launch often marks the start of the marketing program.

Main media

Traditional advertising venues—television, radio, newspaper, magazine and outdoor advertising. Also known as 'above-the-line advertising'.

Marketing message

The key message that an organisation wants to convey about their product or service through a sponsorship.

Media sponsorship

An advertising package generally consisting of paid and/or contra advertising, unpaid promotion and/or editorial support and exclusivity.

Merchandising

The creation of promotional items around an event that will then be sold or given away. Merchandise can be produced and distributed by either the event, the sponsor or both.

Naming rights sponsorship

This is basically the same as a principle sponsorship with the added benefit of the sponsor having their name added to the event name (e.g. the Blockbuster Bowl or the Fosters Melbourne Cup). Also known as 'title sponsorship'.

Narrowcasting

This is the opposite of broadcasting, that is, marketing to a tightly defined group. Also known as 'niche marketing'.

Niche marketing

Targeting a group of people with a very tightly defined set of demographic and/or psychographic characteristics. Also known as 'narrowcasting'.

Offer

The proposal offered to a potential sponsor. Also known as the 'package'.

Official supplier

A (usually) low-level sponsorship in which the sponsor either provides a product or services to the event free or at a substantial discount, often not paying any additional sponsorship fee; or pays a sponsorship fee to secure a guarantee from the sponsee that they will purchase the sponsor's product or service exclusively.

On-pack

The promotion of a sponsorship on the sponsor's actual product packaging. Often done in conjunction with 'in-pack' promotion.

On-selling

A sponsor reselling portions of the purchased sponsor benefits to one or more other companies. This is usually done with the full knowledge and approval of the sponsee.

Outdoor

Above-the-line advertising that takes place outdoors, such as billboards, posters and taxi or bus signage.

Package

The proposal offered to a potential sponsor. Also known as the 'offer'.

Packaging

Structuring the sponsoring benefits and their relationship to the event and the sponsee.

Perimeter signage

Banners and/or signs that are located near an event but not inside the boundaries of the event itself.

Philanthropy

The voluntary giving of funds by foundations, trusts, bequests, corporations or individuals to support human welfare in its broadest sense.

Point-of-difference

The characteristic(s) that set an event, sponsorship, company or product apart from its otherwise similar competition.

Point-of-sale (POS) material

A display, signage or promotional item produced for display with a product in the store and designed to create excitement and differentiate the product from its competitors.

Principal sponsor

This is the pre-eminent sponsor of any event or property, receiving the highest level of benefits and promotion.

Promoter

An individual or company who takes on some of the financial risk as well as responsibility for the marketing and promotion of the event in exchange for a portion of the profits.

Property

This term is used as a generic term for 'sponsee'.

Proposal

The sponsorship offer in written form.

Public relations

Editorial media coverage (i.e. newspaper and magazine articles, television and radio coverage) generally in news, current affairs or lifestyle programming. Also known as 'publicity'.

Publicist

A specialist in gaining editorial media coverage.

Publicity

Editorial media coverage (i.e. newspaper and magazine articles, television and radio coverage) generally in news, current affairs or lifestyle programming. Also known as 'public relations'.

Quantification

Evaluation of the results of the sponsorship program.

Reach

Media term referring to the proportion of the target market that has the opportunity to see or hear any one advertisement. It is expressed as a percentage of the total target market. Also known as 'coverage'.

Reporting

The ongoing process of providing a sponsor with information regarding the performance of their sponsorship against agreed marketing objectives.

Sales promotion

Activities employed to encourage customers to buy a product or differentiate a product from the competition at the point of sale.

Sales sponsorship

A sponsorship that is entered into primarily to gain direct sales (e.g. a brewer sponsoring a festival in order to secure exclusive pouring rights or a hotel chain sponsoring a touring stage show to guarantee all of those room bookings).

Servicing

The process of providing benefits to a sponsor, both what is agreed and additional benefits to assist them in achieving their objectives. Servicing also encompasses strong two-way

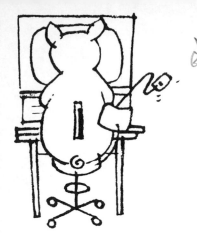

communication between the sponsor and sponsee, as well as reporting.

Signage	Signs that are specific to an event, such as banners, A-frames, scoreboards etc. These can either feature the marketing message of the sponsor, the event, or both.
Sponsee	The recipient of the sponsor's primary sponsorship investment (the fee). Typically, sponsees will fall into the categories of arts, cause, education, community service, event, individual, Internet site, sport or venue.
Sponsor	The organisation that buys sponsorship rights, packaged and granted by the sponsee.
Sponsorship	An investment in sport, community or government activities, the arts, a cause, individual or broadcast which yields a commercial return for the sponsor. The investment can be made in financial, material or human terms.
Sponsorship audit	The assessment of each component of a sponsor's sponsorship portfolio against stringent selection criteria, usually leading to a readjustment of the portfolio.
Sponsorship guidelines	A document produced by sponsors that provides potential sponsees with information on the objectives, target markets, parameters, scope and categories of sponsorship investments made by a company.
Sponsorship plan	A detailed plan that documents how a sponsorship will be serviced and implemented by the sponsee.
Sponsorship policy	A document that indicates an organisation's philosophy and approach to sponsorship, including why they are involved, key influences to the sponsorship process and any sponsorship exclusions or limitations.
Sponsorship strategy	A formal document produced by a company or organisation that outlines the target markets, objectives for sponsorship and specific strategies to achieve these goals. This document is usually closely linked to an organisation's marketing and/or revenue raising strategies. Generally, both sponsors and sponsees will have sponsorship strategies in place.
Target audience	The most appropriate audience for a particular product, service or event. The audience can be made up of one or several target markets, which can sometimes be quite diverse.
Target market	A group of people who are likely purchasers of a product or service, or who are strong candidates for attending an event, and who share a similar demographic and/or psychographic profile.

TARP (Target Audience Rating Point)

Media term referring to the percentage of the target market reached over the course of an advertising campaign. It is a gross measure, taking into account both reach (the number of people that your message reaches) and frequency.

Title sponsor

This is basically the same as a principal sponsorship with the added benefit of the sponsor having their name added to the event name (e.g. the Blockbuster Bowl or the Fosters Melbourne Cup). Also known as 'naming rights sponsor'.

Resources

Associations

We have put together this list of resources to assist you with skill building, research, and developing your networks. This is by no means an exhaustive list but should provide a strong base to get you started. Please note, we have not accepted any fees or special consideration from any of these organisations.

Multinational

International Festivals & Events Association (IFEA)

The IFEA is aimed straight at events and festival organisers with conferences, publications and even a certificate program. For details, contact: IFEA, PO Box 2950, Port Angeles WA 98362 USA, (360) 457 3141, (360) 452 4695 fax or www.ifea.com.

International Association of Business Communicators (IABC)

While the IABC isn't directly related to sponsorship, it is a terrific resource for the media relations aspect of any sponsorship program. They have a searchable database, a lot of publications and experts on hand, and chapters around the world. For details, contact: IABC in the United States, (415) 433 3400, (415) 362 8762 fax or www.iabc.com.

North America

American Marketing Association

This is the top marketing association in the United States. In the absence of a dedicated association for sponsorship professionals, they may be a good resource for you for both education and networking. For details, contact the American Marketing Association, 250 South Wacker Drive, Chicago IL 60606-5819 USA, (312) 648 0536, (312) 993 7542 fax, www.ama.org.

Canadian Public Relations Society Inc.

This association has a wide range of resources and educational programs across Canada. For details, contact CPRS, 220 Laurier Avenue West, Suite 720, Ottawa ONT K1P 5Z9 Canada, (613) 232 1222, (613) 232 0565 fax or www.cprs.ca.

Foundation Center

The Foundation Center focuses squarely on philanthropic grants as opposed to sponsorship. If this is a component of your funding plan, this organisation has a lot to offer. For details, contact the Foundation Center, 79 Fifth Avenue, New York NY 1003-3076 USA, (212) 620 4230, (212) 691 1828 fax or www.fdncenter.org.

Europe

European Sponsorship Consultants' Association (ESCA)

This association caters exclusively to sponsorship consultants. If you are a consultant doing business in Europe, they are probably worth a look. For details, contact ESCA, 2 High Street, Chesham, Buckinghamshire HP5 1EP UK, (44-1494) 791 760 phone/fax or www.sponsorship.org.

Chartered Institute of Marketing

This is a very large and active asssociation, with 60 000 members across the UK. For details, contact CIM, Moor Hall, Cookham, Maidenhead, Berkshire SL6 9QH UK, (44-1628) 427 500, (44-1628) 427 499 fax, www.cim-co.uk.

Institute of Sport Sponsorship (ISS)

This organisation seems to accept membership mainly from sponsors and consultants. Nevertheless, they do have a number of publications and other resources that could be of use to sponsorship seekers. For more information, contact ISS, Warwick House, 25–27 Buckingham Palace Road, London SW1P 0PP UK (44-171) 233 7747, (44-171) 828 7099 fax or www.sports-sponsorship.co.uk.

Australia/New Zealand

Australasian Sponsorship Marketing Association, Inc. (ASMA)

ASMA is one of the world's only non-profit associations for sponsorship marketers, serving professionals from all aspects of the business. For details, contact ASMA, PO Box 11, Seaforth NSW 2092 Australia, (61-2) 9949 9436, (61-2) 9949 9437 fax, asma@ozemail.com.au.

Australian Marketing Institute

The AMI has chapters in major cities, a good conference every year and a lot of education programs and activities. For details, contact AMI, 1800 240 264, 1800 241 264 fax or www.ami.org.au.

South Africa
Institute of Marketing Management

This organisation provides a wide range of marketing, education and networking opportunities. For details, contact IMM, PO Box 91 820, Auckland Park 2006, South Africa, (27-11) 482 1419, (27-11) 726 3639 fax or www.imm.co.sa.

Publications

Multinational
IEG Sponsorship Report

This no frills, bi-weekly newsletter is known for having the most current information, featuring the best and most successful ideas from across the industry, not just the big players. As a subscriber, you will gain access to an international directory of events, the *IEG Legal Guide to Sponsorship* and numerous other publications. For more information, contact IEG, 640 North La Salle, Suite 600, Chicago IL 60610 USA, (312) 944 1727, (312) 789 6488 fax or www.sponsorship.com.

North America
Advertising Age

This is one of the two most popular weekly advertising and marketing publications in North America (*Adweek* is the other). *Advertising Age* will give you a strong, up-to-date understanding of corporations' marketing and advertising initiatives. For details, contact the Advertising Age Group, Subscriber Services, 965 East Jefferson Avenue, Detroit MI 48207-3187 USA, (313) 446 0450, (313) 446 6777 fax or www.adage.com.

Adweek

The benefits of *Adweek* are very similar to those of the *Advertising Age*. The formats are a bit different, however. Check them both out and decide which you prefer. *Adweek* also has several directories and reports available. For details, contact Adweek, 1515 Broadway, New York NY 10036 USA, (800) 722 6658 or www.adweek.com.

American Demographics

American Demographics is the acknowledged bible of market research in North America but that doesn't mean that overseas users won't get a lot out of them as well. Their Web site has a searchable database and great links to government sites. For details, contact American Demographics, 127 West State Street, Ithaca NY 14850 USA, (607) 273 6343, (607) 273 3196 fax or www.demographics.com.

Brandweek

Although similar in format to its sister publication, *Adweek, Brandweek's* focus is squarely on below-the-line marketing activities. Sponsorship, sales promotion, relationship marketing, co-promotions—you name it, they cover it and do it well. For more information, contact Brandweek, 1515 Broadway, 12th Floor, New York NY 10036 USA, (212) 536 5336, (212) 536 1416 fax or www.brandweek.com.

Marketing Magazine

This is Canada's main weekly marketing and advertising magazine. It is very comprehensive and their Web site features excellent links. For details, contact Maclean Hunter Business Publishing, 777 Bay Street, Toronto Ontario M5W 1A7 Canada or www.marketingmag.com.

PROMO

This publication bills itself as *the* magazine of promotional marketing and is very good. They also have a very complete Web site and a searchable archive of articles. For details, contact PROMO through their Web site www.promomagazine.com.

The Sponsorship Report

This monthly publication has been covering Canada's sponsorship industry for some time and is worth a look. For details, contact The Sponsorship Report, 61 Wolfrey Avenue, Toronto M4K K9 Canada, (416) 466 4714, (416) 466 7770 fax or www.sponsorship.ca.

Sports Business Daily

This is actually more of a clipping service, taking sports business articles from a number of newspapers and other publications and delivering them to you daily by e-mail. For more information, contact Sports Business Daily, 12 South Main Street, Suite 401, South Norwalk CT 06854 USA, (203) 838 0800, (203) 857 5590 fax or www.sportsbizdaily.com.

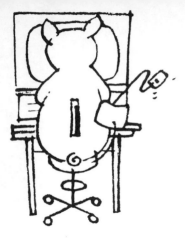

Europe
Debrief

This is a monthly compilation of below-the-line activity in the United Kingdom, aimed primarily at senior marketers. For details, contact The Scott-Smith Partnership, Brokesbourne, Great Whelnetham, Suffolk 1P30 0TY UK or www.debrief.co.uk.

Marketing

This is probably the United Kingdom's pre-eminent marketing publication. It comes out weekly and has a money-back guarantee. For details, contact Marketing on (44-181) 841 3970 or www.marketing.haynet.com.

Sport Business

This large format publication is so slick it would be easy to jump to the conclusion that it is all flash and no substance. Fortunately, that is not the case. It is a very good resource with strong international coverage. For details, contact Sport Business, 205 Blackfriars Foundry, 156 Blackfriars Road, London SE1 8EN UK, (44-171) 721 7161, (44-171) 721 7162 fax or www.sportbusiness.com

Asia
Adweek Asia

The very successful *Adweek* formula has now crossed the Pacific. The coverage is primarily Hong Kong, Singapore and Malaysia. For details, contact Adweek Asia, 2205 Kinwick Centre, 32 Hollywood Road, Central, Hong Kong, (852) 2854 9555, (852) 2854 9336 fax or www.asianad.com.

Australia/New Zealand
B&T

This weekly marketing news publication is pretty good at keeping you on top of what is happening with advertising agencies and major corporations. If you are a sponsee or consultant in Australia, it is a must read as it will give you some insight as to the positioning, wins and failures of your potential sponsors. For details contact Reed Business Information, Locked Bag 2999, Chatswood NSW 2067 Australia, (61-2) 9422 2999, (61-2) 422 2949 fax or www.bandt.com.au.

Professional Marketing

This is the bi-monthly sister publication to *B&T* and is distributed free with your *B&T* subscription. It is very strategy oriented and can provide some good skill building. For details contact Reed Business Information, Locked Bag 2999, Chatswood NSW 2067 Australia, (61-2) 9422 2999, (61-2) 422 2949 fax.

Marketing Magazine

This is New Zealand's top marketing magazine. Published every month except January, it features special sections in each issue. For more information contact Marketing Magazine, PO Box 5544, Auckland, New Zealand, (64-9) 630 8940 or (64-9) 630 1046 fax.

New Zealand Events Update

This monthly publication provides short overviews and contact details for sponsorship opportunities across New Zealand. It also covers industry news and events. For details contact New Zealand Events Update, PO Box 37479, Parnell, Auckland, New Zealand, (64-9) 302 0405, (64-9) 302 4049 fax.

Conferences/seminars

Although there are a number of commercial conference companies that do run sponsorship conferences, because they are not intrinsically involved in the sponsorship industry the quality of them can be patchy. Instead, we have elected to provide the details for established conferences run by recognised industry organisations.

Multinational

International Festivals and Events Association Conferences

IFEA holds conferences and seminars around the world and on a number of different themes, usually very well attended by a great cross-section of festival and event organisers. For details, contact IFEA, PO Box 2950, Port Angeles WA 98362 USA, (360) 457 3141, (360) 452 4695 fax or www.ifea.com.

Smart Marketing Streetwise Workshops

These skills workshops, presented by the authors of this book, are available in many countries. Courses can also be tailored for your specific needs. For details, contact

SMSW (Asia-Pacific), 78 Dickson St, Newtown NSW 2042 Australia, (61-2) 9565 4660, (61-2) 9565 4670 fax or SMSW (North America), 4306 Wakefield Dr, Annandale VA 22003 USA, (703) 323 6480 (phone or fax), or www.smsw.com.

North America
IEG Sponsorship Seminar

This huge conference is held every March in Chicago. It brings together fifteen hundred sponsors and sponsees from around the world for three intense days of education and networking. For more information, contact IEG, 640 North La Salle, Suite 600, Chicago IL 60610 USA, (312) 944 1727, (312) 789 6488 fax or www.sponsorship.com.

International Sport Summit

All facets of sports business are covered including marketing, production, industrial relations, management, licensing and lobbying. For details, contact EJ Krause & Associates, 6550 Rock Spring Drive, Suite 500, Bethesda MD 20817 USA, (301) 493 5500, (301) 493 5705 fax, or www.ejkrause.com.

Europe
National Sponsorship Conference (UK)

This is the annual National Sponsorship Conference for the United Kingdom and is usually held early in the year. For more information, contact BDS Sponsorship on (44) 171 240 3252 or (44) 171 240 3243 fax.

Research

Research is a large part of preparing any sponsorship document. Below you will find a number of excellent resources for background research.

General
ABI/Inform Full Text Online

Provides the full text of articles from hundreds of publications worldwide. You can print them out or download articles onto your own disk. This service is typically found at universities and business reference libraries.

Business Periodicals On-Disk (BPO)

This is not widely available but it is well worth finding. It is a CD-ROM-based listing of all of the articles for hundreds of publications worldwide, similar to ABI/Inform. The beauty is that you get the actual article, as printed, including photographs and graphics. We have found the best access to this service at universities.

The Electric Library

http://www.elibrary.com

If you are on the Web, this is a good option. You can search for articles on keywords, exactly like ABI/Inform, and download them to your own computer. Most of their publications are consumer, not business, oriented, but they are adding publications all the time.

International Events Group (IEG)

US-based IEG probably does more in the area of sponsorship research than any other single organisation. Their databases of sponsor and sponsee information are vast, up to date and very useful. For more information on what is available, contact IEG, 640 North La Salle, Suite 600, Chicago IL 60610 USA, (312) 944 1727, (312) 789 6488 fax or www.sponsorship.com.

Brian Sweeney & Associates

This organisation does an annual survey of Australians, determining their interest and participation in sports and cultural activities, their attitudes about sponsorship and their recall of specific sponsors. For more information, contact Brian Sweeney & Associates, 232 Dorcas Street, South Melbourne VIC 3205 Australia, (61-3) 9699 8466, (61-3) 9690 7543 fax.

US Government Sources

➤ American Statistics Index
➤ ASI Abstracts
➤ US Census

General Business Sources

➤ Encyclopedia of Business Information Sources
➤ Gale Research

➤ Business Information Sources

➤ Standard and Poor's Industry Surveys

➤ Predicasts F & S Index—United States

➤ Predicasts F & S Index—Europe

➤ Business Periodicals Index

➤ Consumer's Index

➤ Thomas Register

➤ Statistical Reference Index

Corporate profiles

International Events Group

See IEG information above.

Hoover's Online

http://www.hoovers.com

This is a great resource for finding profiles of American companies and industries. This is not a free service, but they do let you try it out before committing.

Prospect Research Online

http://www.rpbooks.com

A subscription service with over one thousand US and three hundred Canadian corporate profiles that will assist non-profit organisations in gaining sponsorship. Also provides biographies, major gift announcements and special interest group articles. Ask for their on-line ten-minute tour.

Media

The following publications may assist you in understanding the range of media available to you and matching your organisation with appropriate media outlets, both for public relations and sponsorship. Most of them are available on-line, making it easy to determine their appropriateness.

Broadcasting and Cablecasting Yearbook

Contact your local business reference library for details on this publication.

Editor & Publisher International

This is the long time bible of the newspaper industry. For details, contact Editor & Publisher Co., 11 West 19th Street, New York NY 10011-4234 USA, (212) 675 4380, (212) 929 1894 fax or www.mediainfo.com/emedia.

Gale's Directory of Publications and Broadcast Media

For details, contact Gale Research, 835 Penobscot Building, Detroit, MI 48226, (800) 877 4253, (800) 414 5043 fax.

Margaret Gee's Media Guide

This is a great handbook and a must-have for people carrying out publicity in Australia. It is updated regularly. For details, contact Information Australia, 45 Flinders Lane, Melbourne Vic. 3000 Australia, (61-3) 9654 2800, (61-3) 9650 5261 fax, or www.infoaust.com.

Media Central

For details, contact Media Central, 11 Riverbend Drive South, Stamford CT 06907-0225 USA, (203) 358 4134.

| Web sites

Sponsorship, marketing and media sites

Advertising Media Internet Centre

http://www.amic.com

Most features cost dollars to use, but they do have some free benefits.

Advertising World

http://advertising.utexas.edu.world

This site has serious links, probably one of the most complete lists on the Web. It is very focused on the United States but international sites are welcome and listings are free to appropriate companies.

Advertising Age

http://www.AdAge.com

A lot of good information, including up to a dozen articles from each weekly publication and it's available free. The list of articles goes back about two months and features a lot of useful stuff.

Australian Media Facilities Directory

http://www.amfd.com.au

This site features an exhaustive list of anyone and everyone having to do with media, marketing and production, including links to Web sites. If you have an appropriate site, listing it is free.

Brandweek

http://www.brandweek.com

This is the electronic version of the excellent publication, *Brandweek*. It includes a lot of articles, as well as links to sister publications, *Adweek* and *Mediaweek*.

Canadian Advertising Rates & Data

http://www.cardmedia.com

Very complete links to Canadian media organisations and associations.

Canadian News Wire

http://www.newswire.ca

This is a searchable database of press releases from a wide range of Canadian companies and events.

European Sponsorship Consultants' Association (ESCA)

http://www.sponsorship.org

Although this site will be of limited use to sponsorship seekers because of their strong focus on consultants, there may be some good information for you.

IEG Network

http://www.sponsorship.com

This site is all about sponsorship. It is stylish, their information is complete and they do provide free links. They also include a lot of information about their seminars, publications and other activities.

International Festivals and Events Association (IFEA)

http://www.ifea.com

This is a comprehensive site, listing all of the activities and publications for this international organisation.

Philanthropy Journal

http://www.philanthropy-journal.org

Although it is heavily philanthropic in thrust, it is still a reasonably good information source for non-profit organisations. The site does include a great forum, which should be useful for those very new to sponsorship.

PR Newswire

http://www.prnewswire.com

This Web site provides up-to-the-minute news releases from major US corporations and events. It allows you to search all press releases, by company, for the last several years.

Arts and non-profit sites

Although most of these sites are specific to one country or another, don't limit yourself geographically. Many of them feature good advice and links that will be useful to a wide range of cultural and non-profit organisations.

Arts Info

http://www.artsinfo.net.au

This Australian site is an initiative of the Commonwealth Department of Communications and the Arts and has a lot of interesting and useful information, ranging from educational resources to grants to making contacts in Asia.

Arts Wire

http://artswire.org

This is a site put up by the New York Foundation for the Arts. It is a service specifically for cultural institutions and includes 'Current', a good on-line publication, as well as terrific cultural links.

ArtsUSA

http://www.artsusa.org

This is a very interesting and very complete site run by the American Council for the Arts. It includes a lot of information on programs, education and policy, and has some excellent links.

Australia Council Research

http://www.ozco.gov.au/publicat/Reslist.htm

This page lists the title and description of all research published by the Australia Council from 1982 through 1996. It includes dozens of research papers on topics ranging from 'Art Galleries: Who goes?' to 'Corporate Support for the Arts: Survey of Expenditure and Attitudes' to 'Older Australians and the Arts'. You will still need to contact the Australia Council directly for the actual studies but this is a great place to find out what is available.

The Non-Profit Times

http://www.nptimes.com

In the on-line version of a real life magazine out of the United States, we found some interesting articles, a good on-line directory and some very useful links.

State of the Arts

http://www.stateart.com.au

A good Australian-based arts site which features a fair amount of sponsorship information.

Sports sites

Business of Sports

www.bizsports.com

This site provides plenty of articles, including an archive, and good links to sporting organisations.

Institute of Sport Sponsorship

www.sports-sponsorship.co.uk

They have limited reference information on-line but the site does overview the organisation really well.

Sport Business

www.sportbusiness.com

This site provides up-to-the-minute news on sports and sponsorship around the world and includes a good, searchable archive.

Sponsorship law

If you do not already have a good sponsorship lawyer, you can contact one of the following organisations for a referral. You will note that most of these organisations are specific to sport but the skills required for sponsorship are quite transferable across a range of sponsorship types. If you are a cultural organisation, festival and so on do not hesitate in contacting these organisations for assistance.

North America

Sports Lawyers Association Inc.

11250 Roger Bacon Drive, Suite 8

Reston VA 20190 USA

(703) 437 4377

(703) 435 4390 fax

Europe

British Association for Sport and Law

School of Law

The Manchester Metropolitan University

Hathersage Road

Manchester M13 0JA UK

(44-161) 247 6445

(44-161) 247 6309 fax

Australia/New Zealand/Asia

Australian & New Zealand Sports Law Association Inc. (ANZSLA)

PO Box 4252

Melbourne University

Parkville Vic. 3052 Australia

(61-3) 9344 6197

(61-3) 9347 2392 fax

Allen Allen & Hemsley

Solicitors and Notaries

GPO Box 50

Sydney NSW 2001 Australia

(61-2) 9230 4000

(61-2) 9230 5333 fax

Lionel Hogg, a Partner at Allen Allen & Hemsley, created the sponsorship agreement pro forma included in Appendix 3. This firm has offices throughout Australia and Asia and is happy to provide expert assistance or referrals to appropriate sponsorship lawyers. You are also welcome to contact Lionel Hogg directly on (61-7) 3334 3170, (61-7) 3334 3444 or lionel.hogg@aahq.com.au.

Sponsorship agreement pro forma

 **Legal1.doc**

| Warning

This document is provided as a sample only and is not a substitute for legal advice. You should seek the advice of a suitably qualified and experienced lawyer before using this document. In particular, you or your lawyer should:

➤ Check the law in your jurisdiction—make sure this agreement works there.

➤ Check for changes to the law—law and practice might have altered since this document was drafted or you last checked the situation.

➤ Modify wherever necessary—review this document critically and never use it without first amending it to suit your needs. Remember that every sponsorship is different.

➤ Beware of limits of expertise. If you are not legally qualified or are not familiar with this area of the law, do not use this document without first obtaining legal advice about it.

You should also read the Guidance Notes (page 129) before using this sample agreement.

Sponsorship Agreement

This Sponsorship Agreement comprises the attached Schedules, Special Conditions and Standard Conditions.

Schedules

Schedule 1	
"Sponsor"	

Title: ....

Address: ....

Representative: ....

Telephone: ....

Facsimile: ....

E-mail: ....

Schedule 2	
"Owner"	

(Identify the sponsee – the legal entity receiving the Sponsorship. This must be the proper name of the company or association receiving the funds and controlling the team, event or venue being Sponsored, not the name of the team, event or venue etc.)

Title: ....

Address: ....

Representative: ....

Telephone: ....

Facsimile: ....

E-mail: ....

Schedule 3	
"Commencement Date"	

(Insert when the Sponsorship starts.)

....

Schedule 4	
"Term"	

(Insert when the Sponsorship will end or for how long it will last e.g. "5 years".)

....
....
....
....

Schedule 5

Option to renew

See clause 1.5.
Does Sponsor have an option to renew?
Yes/No
If yes:
- *for what "Period" (specify an extended finishing date or further term, e.g. 3 years)?*
- *will the sponsorship fee and other Owner Benefits be the same after renewal? If not, list the new benefits.*

....
....
....
....
....
....
....

Schedule 6

First right of refusal

See clause 1.6.
Does Sponsor have a first right of refusal?
Yes/No

....
....
....
....

Schedule 7

"Property"

Identify the event, team, venue or other property the subject of this sponsorship.

....
....
....
....

Schedule 8

"Sponsorship Category"

Identify the nature of the sponsorship (e.g. title/category/official supplier etc.).

....
....
....
....

Schedule 9

"Territory"

Specify the area in which the sponsorship operates (e.g. state, region, country, continent, worldwide, etc.).

....
....
....
....

Schedule 10

Sponsor objectives

See clause 2.1.
Be specific (list bottom-line sales objectives, measurable promotional activities, business development targets, etc.).

1. ....
2. ....
3. ....

Schedule 11

Owner objectives

See clause 2.2.
Be specific (list expected leverage from Sponsor in developing event/sport, target participation or attendance numbers, entry fee and merchandise income, measurable business development targets, etc.).

1. ....
2. ....
3. ....

Schedule 12

"Sponsor Benefits"

List, in detail, the signage/tickets/ hospitality/advertising credits/ merchandising rights and other benefits that Owner must provide to Sponsor (be precise about amounts, timing etc.).

1. ....
2. ....
3. ....
4. ....
5. ....
6. ....
7. ....
8. ....
9. ....
10. ....

Schedule 13

"Owner Benefits"

List, in detail, the sponsorship fee, contra/in-kind benefits that Sponsor must provide to Owner (be precise about amounts, timing, etc.).

1. ....
2. ....
3. ....
4. ....
5. ....
6. ....
7. ....
8. ....
9. ....
10. ....

Schedule 14

Evaluation criteria

See clause 8.3.
- *Is media analysis required and, if so, by whom, at whose expense, how regularly and what details must be provided?*
- *Is Owner obliged to provide reports on mutual marketing activities, demographic information, samples of printed and promotional materials and, if so, what and when?*
- *Specify, in detail, the level of performance (and how it will be assessed) which is regarded by Sponsor as unacceptable.*
- *Specify the consequences of failing to achieve this level (e.g. right of termination, reduced fees or benefits).*
- *Specify the level of performance (and how it will be assessed) above which Sponsor's reasonable expectations are exceeded.*
- *Specify the consequences of this level of performance (e.g. increased sponsorship fee or benefits).*
- *Specify any other relevant evaluation criteria, information or consequences.*

....
....
....
....
....
....
....
....
....
....
....
....
....
....
....
....

Schedule 15

"Applicable law"

Identify the country or state the laws of which will apply to this Agreement.

....
....
....
....

Schedule 16

"Owner Marks"

Insert here all trade marks, names, logos, etc. which Sponsor is entitled to use under this Agreement. Include artwork. If nothing is listed, Sponsor may use all Owner Marks.

....
....
....
....
....

Schedule 17

"Sponsor Marks"

Insert here all trade marks, names, logos, etc. which Owner is entitled to use under this Agreement. Include artwork. If nothing is listed, Owner may use all Sponsor Marks.

....
....
....
....
....
....

Schedule 18

Use of Owner Marks

See clause 5.1.
List here the specific purposes for which
Owner Marks can be used by Sponsor.

1. ....
2. ....
3. ....

Schedule 19

Use of Sponsor Marks

See clause 5.1.
List here the specific purposes for which
Sponsor Marks can be used by Owner.

1. ....
2. ....
3. ....

Schedule 20

Promotional and media objectives

See clause 6.3.
Be specific (e.g. list target media outlets,
promotional events, nature of coverage,
etc.).

1. ....
2. ....
3. ....
4. ....
5. ....

Schedule 21

Competitors of Sponsor

See clauses 7.1 and 21.3.

1. ....
2. ....
3. ....

Schedule 22

Competitors of Property

See clauses 7.2 and 21.3.

1. ....
2. ....
3. ....

Schedule 23

Sponsor's termination events

See clause 9.2.
Insert here the circumstances in which
Sponsor can terminate this Agreement.

1. ....
2. ....
3. ....
4. ....
5. ....

Schedule 24

Owner's termination events

*See clause 9.3.
Insert here the circumstances in which Owner can terminate this Agreement.*

1. ....
2. ....
3. ....
4. ....
5. ....

Schedule 25

Insurance

*See clause 16.
Insert here the amount of public liability insurance required to be maintained by Owner and full details of any other insurance, such as event cancellation insurance or product liability insurance for the manufacture or sale of licensed merchandise, required for the purposes of this Agreement.*

1. Public liability—amount.

....

....

2. Other:

....

....

....

Schedule 26

Ambush strategies

*See clause 8.1.
Include here specific strategies designed to minimise the likelihood of Ambush occurring, such as obligations on Owner to:*
- *prevent or minimise Competitor involvement;*
- *exercise control of venue access and signage;*
- *impose contractual obligations on bidders for commercial rights not to engage in Ambushing should the bids be unsuccessful;*
- *negotiate broadcasting agreements to provide Sponsor with a first right of refusal to take category exclusive advertising time during broadcasts of the event;*
- *impose ticketing restrictions;*
- *prevent the re-use of tickets or licensed products as prize giveaways;*
- *provide sponsorship fee rebates (be very specific) if serious Ambush occurs, etc.*

1. ....
2. ....
3. ....
4. ....
5. ....

Special conditions

Insert here any changes to the Standard Conditions and any special conditions not referred to in the Standard Conditions or the Schedules.

....

....

....

Standard conditions

1 Sponsorship

1.1 EXCLUSIVITY

Sponsor shall be the exclusive sponsor of the Property, in the Sponsorship Category, in the Territory.

1.2 TERM

Subject to this Agreement, the sponsorship starts on the Commencement Date and is effective for the Term.

1.3 CONSIDERATION

The consideration for this Agreement is the mutual conferring of Benefits referred to in clause 1.4.

1.4 BENEFITS

Sponsor must confer Owner Benefits on Owner, and Owner must confer Sponsor Benefits on Sponsor, at the times outlined in, and in accordance with, Schedules 12 and 13.

1.5 OPTION TO RENEW

(a) This clause applies if the parties specify 'Yes' in Schedule 5.

(b) Sponsor has an option to renew this Agreement for the further Period specified in Schedule 5 if:
- Sponsor is not in breach under this Agreement; and
- Sponsor gives notice in writing to Owner no fewer than 3 months before the end of the Term stating it intends to exercise the option.

(c) If Sponsor exercises the option, the provisions of this Agreement (except for this clause 1.5) shall continue in full force and effect for the further Period, subject to any differences in fees or Owner Benefits specified in Schedule 5 for the further Period.

1.6 FIRST RIGHT OF REFUSAL

(a) This clause applies if the parties specify 'Yes' in Schedule 6.

(b) Owner must not enter into an agreement with any other person to sponsor the Property in the Sponsorship Category at or immediately after the end of the Term without first offering the sponsorship to Sponsor on the same terms as it proposes to offer

to (or as have been offered by) other parties.

(c) If Sponsor declines within 30 days to accept the new sponsorship terms, Owner may enter into an agreement with a third party, but only on the terms offered to, and rejected by, Sponsor.

(d) Sponsor's first right of refusal extends to any revised terms offered to or by third parties after Sponsor declines to accept the initial terms.

1.7 NO ASSIGNMENT

(a) Sponsor must not assign, charge or otherwise deal with Sponsor Benefits without the prior written consent of Owner.

(b) Owner must not assign, charge or otherwise deal with Owner Benefits without the prior written consent of Sponsor.

(c) This clause does not apply to Owner Benefits or Sponsor Benefits that the parties, on signing this Agreement, agree will be conferred on third parties.

2 Objectives

2.1 OBJECTIVES OF SPONSOR

The primary objectives of the Sponsor in entering into this Agreement are:
- to associate Sponsor's brand with the Property;
- to promote the products and services of Sponsor;
- to encourage brand loyalty to Sponsor;
- to assist in raising and maintaining Sponsor's corporate profile and image;
- to provide to Sponsor marketing leverage opportunities related to the Property;
- to promote community awareness of, affinity for and (if relevant) participation in the Property;
- to continually review and evaluate the ongoing success and performance of the sponsorship for maximum commercial advantage to all parties; and
- the objectives outlined in Schedule 10.

2.2 OBJECTIVES OF OWNER

The primary objectives of the Owner in entering into this Agreement are:
- to secure sponsorship funds and other benefits;
- to increase the profile, standing, brand value and (if relevant) participation in the Property;

- to promote the profile and corporate image of Sponsor and the use of Sponsor's products and services;
- to continually review and evaluate the ongoing success and performance of the sponsorship for the maximum commercial advantage to all parties; and
- the objectives outlined in Schedule 11.

2.3 FULFILMENT OF OBJECTIVES

The parties must act at all times in good faith towards each other with a view to fulfilling the objectives outlined in clauses 2.1 and 2.2. This Agreement is to be interpreted in a manner that best satisfies the fulfilment of those objectives.

3 Warranties

3.1 OWNER WARRANTIES

Owner warrants that:
- it has full right and legal authority to enter into and perform its obligations under this Agreement;
- it owns the Property (or, if the Property is not legally capable of being owned, it owns rights which effectively confer unfettered control of the Property);
- Owner Marks do not infringe the trade marks, trade names or other rights of any person;
- it has, or will at the relevant time have, all government licences, permits and other authorities relevant to the Property;
- it will comply with all applicable laws relating to the promotion and conduct of the Property; and
- throughout this Agreement, it will conduct itself so as not to cause detriment, damage, injury or embarrassment to Sponsor.

3.2 SPONSOR WARRANTIES

Sponsor warrants that:
- it has full right and legal authority to enter into and perform its obligations under this Agreement;
- Sponsor Marks do not infringe the trade marks, trade names or other rights of any other person;
- it will comply with all applicable laws in marketing and promoting its sponsorship of the Property; and
- throughout this Agreement, it will conduct itself so as not to cause detriment, damage, injury or embarrassment to the Owner.

4 Disclosure

4.1 INITIAL DISCLOSURE

Owner warrants that it has disclosed to Sponsor:
- the substance (other than financial details) of all agreements entered into or currently under negotiation with Owner for sponsorship, exclusive or preferred supplier status or other like arrangements relating to the Property; and
- all other circumstances which might have a material impact upon Sponsor's decision to enter into this Agreement.

4.2 CONTINUING DISCLOSURE

Owner must from time to time keep Sponsor informed of:
- new sponsorship, exclusive or preferred service or supplier status or

other like arrangements conferred by Owner in respect of the Property;
- significant marketing programs and other promotional activities which might provide leverage opportunities for Sponsor; and
- research and demographic information held or commissioned by Owner about the Property and its participants.

5 Marks and title

5.1 AUTHORISED USE

(a) Sponsor may use Owner Marks:
- for all purposes reasonably incidental to obtaining the Sponsor Benefits; and
- as permitted in Schedule 18.

(b) Owner may use Sponsor Marks:
- for all purposes reasonably incidental to obtaining the Owner Benefits; and
- as permitted in Schedule 19.

5.2 NO UNAUTHORISED USE

Sponsor must not use or permit the use of Owner Marks and Owner must not use or permit the use of Sponsor Marks unless:
- authorised by this Agreement; or
- with the written consent of the other party.

5.3 MERCHANDISE

(a) Unless permitted in Schedule 18, Sponsor must not manufacture, sell or license the manufacture or sale of any promotional or other merchandise bearing Owner Marks without Owner's prior written consent.

(b) Unless permitted in Schedule 19, Owner must not manufacture, sell or license the manufacture or sale of any promotional or other merchandise bearing Sponsor Marks without Sponsor's prior written consent.

(c) All authorised merchandise bearing Owner Marks or Sponsor Marks permitted under this Agreement must be:
- of a high standard;
- of such style, appearance and quality as to suit the best exploitation of the Sponsor, Owner and Property (as the case may be); and
- free from product defects, of merchantable quality and suited for its intended purpose.

5.4 IMAGE

The parties must ensure that any authorised use by them of the other's marks or intellectual property rights:
- is lawful;
- properly and accurately represents those rights;
- is consistent with the other's corporate image; and
- (if used in connection with the provision of goods or services) is associated only with goods or services of the highest quality.

5.5 ENFORCEMENT PROTECTION

The parties must provide all reasonable assistance to each other to protect against infringers of Owner Marks or Sponsor Marks in connection with the Property.

5.6 TITLE

Despite any rights to use another's marks conferred under this Agreement:

- Owner holds all legal and equitable right, title and interest in and to the Property and all Owner Marks;
- Sponsor holds all legal and equitable right, title and interest in and to the Sponsor Marks;
- naming, title and other rights conferred by this Agreement merely constitute licences to use the relevant Owner Marks or Sponsor Marks (as the case may be) for the purposes of, and in accordance with, this Agreement and do not confer any property right or interest in those marks.
- the right to use another's marks is non-exclusive and non-assignable.

5.7 INFRINGEMENTS INCIDENTAL TO TELEVISION BROADCASTS, ETC.

This clause 5 does not prevent any person holding rights to televise or reproduce images associated with the Property from incidentally broadcasting or reproducing Sponsor Marks appearing as or in signage on premises controlled by Owner and relevant to the Property.

5.8 NO ALTERATION TO BROADCAST SIGNAL, ETC.

Owner must not authorise or permit any media rights holder contracted in respect of the Property (e.g. the official broadcaster of an event or an authorised Internet site manager or multimedia provider) in the exercise of its rights to alter any images associated with the Property (e.g. by the artificial electronic insertion, removal or alteration of signage or other images) without the prior written consent of Sponsor.

6 Media, branding, leverage, etc.

6.1 MEDIA EXPOSURE

At all reasonable opportunities:

- Owner will use its best endeavours to obtain public and media exposure of the sponsorship; and
- Sponsor will use its best endeavours to obtain public and media exposure of the Property.

6.2 APPROVAL

Media releases relating to the sponsorship must:

- be issued jointly by the parties; or
- not be issued by one party without the consent of the other.

6.3 PROMOTIONAL OBJECTIVES

Owner and Sponsor must use their best endeavours to achieve their promotional and media objectives outlined in Schedule 20. Sponsor licenses Owner to use Sponsor Marks and Owner licenses Sponsor to use Owner Marks for these purposes.

6.4 LEVERAGE

Sponsor has the right at its cost to:

- promote itself, its brands and its products and services in association with the Property; and
- engage in advertising and promotional activities to maximise the benefits to it of its association with the Property,

provided that it will not knowingly or recklessly engage in any advertising or promotional activities which reflect unfavourably on the Property, the parties or any other sponsors of the Property.

7 Restraints

7.1 OWNER RESTRAINT

Owner must not:

- enter into any sponsorship or supply arrangements for the Property in the Sponsorship Category with any other person; or
- authorise the provision of any products or services to the Property, in any Sponsorship Category, or authorise any association with the Property, by any Competitor of the Sponsor.

7.2 SPONSOR RESTRAINT

Sponsor must not enter into any sponsorship or supply arrangements with any Competitor of the Owner during the Term or within a reasonable time after the end of the Term.

7.3 INJUNCTIONS

The parties acknowledge that the restraints referred to in clauses 7.1 and 7.2 cannot adequately be compensated for in damages and consent to injunctive relief for the enforcement of these restraints.

8 Marketing and service delivery

8.1 MARKETING COMMITTEE

Owner and Sponsor will establish a marketing committee to meet quarterly (or otherwise, as agreed) for the purposes of:

- reviewing the progress of the sponsorship and the mutual rights conferred under this Agreement;
- evaluating the success of the sponsorship against its objectives;
- discussing further opportunities for leverage and cross-promotional activities;
- maximising the ongoing benefits to the parties, implementing promotional strategies for the parties and identifying new, mutual opportunities; and
- maximising the Sponsor Benefits by:
  - identifying actual or potential Ambush activities;
  - using their best endeavours to prevent Ambush or minimise its potential impact on the sponsorship; and
  - directing implementation of the strategies outlined in Schedule 26.

8.2 SERVICE DELIVERY

Both Sponsor and Owner must designate a representative to be primarily responsible for the provision of the day-to-day service and support required by the other party under this Agreement. Until otherwise nominated, the representatives will be the representatives named in Schedules 1 and 2.

8.3 EVALUATION

The parties must evaluate the success of the sponsorship in accordance with the criteria outlined in Schedule 14 and with the consequences (if any) outlined in that Schedule.

9 Termination

9.1 EXPIRY

This Agreement, unless terminated earlier under this clause or extended under clause 1, will continue until the end of the Term.

9.2 EARLY TERMINATION BY SPONSOR

Sponsor may terminate this Agreement if:

- Owner fails to provide a Sponsor Benefit, and failure continues for 7 days after Owner receives written notice from Sponsor to provide the Benefit;
- Owner suffers an Insolvency occurrence;
- any event outlined in Schedule 23 occurs;
- application of the evaluation criteria in Schedule 14 permits termination;
- any laws come into operation which in any way restrict, prohibit or otherwise regulate the sponsorship of, or association by Sponsor with, the Property so that the benefits available to Sponsor are materially reduced or altered or Sponsor's obligations under this Agreement are materially increased;
- for reasons beyond the reasonable control of Sponsor, Sponsor is unable to continue to exploit and enjoy fully the Sponsor Benefits;
- any major, public controversy arises in connection with the Owner, the Property or this Agreement which, in the reasonable opinion of Sponsor, reflects adversely and substantially on Sponsor's corporate image;
- any statement, representation or warranty made by Owner in connection with this Agreement proves to have been incorrect or misleading in any material respect;
- the rights conferred on Sponsor under this Agreement are directly or indirectly diminished, prejudiced or compromised in any way by the reckless acts or omissions of Owner;
- Owner has not used its best endeavours to ensure that the exclusive rights conferred on Sponsor under this Agreement are not directly or indirectly diminished, prejudiced or compromised in any way by the acts or omissions of third parties (e.g. by Ambush).

9.3 EARLY TERMINATION BY OWNER

Owner may terminate this Agreement if:

- Sponsor fails to provide a material Sponsor Benefit, and failure continues for 7 days after Sponsor receives written notice from Owner to provide the benefit;
- Sponsor suffers an Insolvency occurrence;
- any event outlined in Schedule 24 occurs;
- any major, public controversy arises in connection with the Sponsor or this Agreement which, in the reasonable opinion of Owner, revokes adversely and substantially on Owner's corporate image or upon the Property;
- any statement, representation or warranty made by Sponsor in connection with this Agreement proves to have been incorrect or misleading in any material respect when made;
- the rights conferred on Owner under this Agreement are directly or indirectly diminished, prejudiced or compromised in any way by the reckless acts or omissions of Sponsor.

9.4 IMMATERIAL BREACHES

Nothing in this clause entitles a party to terminate this Agreement for trivial or immaterial breaches which cannot be remedied, however, this does not prevent termination for regular, consistent or repeated breaches (even if they would, alone, be trivial or immaterial).

9.5 METHOD OF TERMINATION

A party entitled to terminate this Agreement may do so by notice in writing to the other at the address specified in Schedule 1 or Schedule 2, as the case may be.

9.6 EFFECT OF EARLY TERMINATION

Termination of this Agreement for any reason shall be without prejudice to the rights and obligations of each party accrued up to and including the date of termination.

10 Rebranding

10.1 CHANGE OF NAME, LOGO, PRODUCT, ETC.

If at any time Sponsor changes its name or logo, or wishes to change any Sponsor's product associated with Property, Sponsor may rebrand the sponsorship of the Property provided that, in the reasonable opinion of Owner, to do so will not affect the good name and image of the Property or Owner.

10.2 COSTS

Rebranding must be at Sponsor's cost. This includes:

- direct costs to Sponsor; and
- any costs incurred by Owner directly or indirectly resulting from the rebranding.

11 Governing law

This Agreement is governed by and must be construed in accordance with the Applicable Law.

12 No partnership joint venture agency, etc.

Nothing in this Agreement shall be construed to place the parties in a relationship of partnership, joint venture or principal and agent.

13 Ongoing assistance

Each party must promptly:

- do all things;
- sign all documents; and
- provide all relevant assistance and information, reasonably required by the other party to enable the performance by the parties of their obligations under this Agreement.

14 Costs

14.1 OWN COSTS

Each party must pay its own costs of and incidental to the negotiation, preparation and execution of this Agreement.

14.2 SIGNAGE, ETC.

Unless otherwise specified as a Sponsor Benefit or Owner Benefit, each party must pay its own advertising, leverage, general overhead and incidental costs related to the performance of its obligations under this Agreement. Despite this, all signage, artwork, photography, film, video tape and similar expenses directly or indirectly incurred under this Agreement must be met by Sponsor unless otherwise provided for in the Schedule or Special Conditions.

15 Notices

Notices under this Agreement may be delivered or sent by post, facsimile or e-mail to the relevant addresses outlined in Schedules 1 and 2 (as the case may be) and will be deemed to have been received in the ordinary course of delivery of notices in that form.

16 Insurance

16.1 LIABILITY INSURANCE

Owner must effect and keep current:
- a public liability insurance policy for an amount not less than the amount specified in Schedule 25 for any single claim for liability of Owner or Sponsor or both for death, personal injury or property damage occasioned to any person in respect of the Property (including a contractual liability endorsement to cover the obligations of Owner under clause 17);
- such other insurance as is specified in Schedule 25; and
- if Property is a one-off event (or if the parties specify in Schedule 25), event cancellation insurance in an amount equalling or exceeding the value of Sponsor Benefits.

16.2 PRODUCT LIABILITY INSURANCE

If:
- Owner is authorised under this Agreement to manufacture, sell or license the sale or manufacture of any merchandise bearing Sponsor Marks; or
- Sponsor is authorised under this Agreement to manufacture, sell or license the sale or manufacture of any merchandise bearing Owner Marks;

the party so authorised must effect and keep current a product liability insurance policy for an amount not less than the amount specified in Schedule 25 for any single claim for liability of Owner or Sponsor or both for death, personal injury or property damage occasioned to any person in respect of the manufacture or sale of the merchandise (e.g. for claims relating to a defective product).

16.3 TERMS OF POLICIES

All insurance policies effected under this Agreement must:
- be wholly satisfactory to the Beneficiary;
- identify the Beneficiary as a named insured;
- remain enforceable for the benefit of the Beneficiary even if invalid or unenforceable against Payer; and
- include full, automatic reinstatement cover at all times during the Term.

16.4 OTHER OBLIGATIONS

The Payer must:
- not violate, or permit the violation of, any conditions of these policies; and
- provide insurance certificates and copies of the policies to the Beneficiary on its reasonable request.

16.5 DEFINITIONS

In this clause 16:
- "Beneficiary" means the party for whose benefit an insurance policy must be effected under this clause;
- "Payer" means the party obliged to effect an insurance policy under this clause.

17 Indemnities

17.1 OWNER INDEMNITIES

Owner must indemnify Sponsor and Sponsor's officers, employees and agents from and against all claims, damages, liabilities, losses and expenses related to:
- any breach by Owner of this Agreement;
- the inaccuracy of any warranty or representations made by Owner;
- any act or omission by Owner in its performance of this Agreement; and
- liabilities for which insurance is required under clause 16.

17.2 SPONSOR INDEMNITIES

Sponsor must indemnify Owner and Owner's officers, employees and agents from and against all claims, damages, liabilities, losses and expenses related to:
- any breach by Sponsor of this Agreement;
- the inaccuracy of any warranty or representations made by Sponsor;
- any act or omission by Sponsor in its performance of this Agreement; and
- all liabilities for which insurance is required under clause 16.

18 Dispute resolution

18.1 MEDIATION

Any dispute or difference about this Agreement must be resolved as follows:-
- the parties must first refer the dispute to mediation by an agreed accredited mediator or, failing agreement, by a person appointed by the President or other senior officer of the Law Society or Bar Association in the jurisdiction of the Applicable Law;
- the mediator must determine the rules of the mediation if the parties do not agree;
- mediation commences when a party gives written notice to the other specifying the dispute and requiring its resolution under this clause;
- the parties must negotiate in good faith to resolve the dispute within 14 days; and
- any information or documents obtained through or as part of the mediation must not be used for any purpose other than the settlement of the dispute.

18.2 FINAL RESOLUTION

If the dispute is not resolved within 14 days of the notice of its commencement, either party may then, but not earlier, commence legal proceedings in an appropriate court.

18.3 CONTRACT PERFORMANCE

Each party must continue to perform this Agreement despite the existence of a dispute or any proceedings under this clause.

18.4 EXCEPTIONS TO MEDIATION

Nothing in this clause prevents:

- a party from seeking urgent injunctive relief in respect of an actual or apprehended breach of this Agreement;
- Sponsor from exercising its rights under the first 3 sub-paragraphs of clause 9.2; or
- Owner from exercising its rights under the first 3 sub-paragraphs of clause 9.3.

19 Confidentiality

The commercial terms of this Agreement are confidential to the parties unless they otherwise agree. However, this does not prevent:

- Sponsor or Owner disclosing the existence or the sponsorship to the general public; or
- any promotional, marketing or sponsorship activities authorised or required under this Agreement.

20 Entire agreement

This Agreement represents the entire agreement between the parties and supersedes all other agreements (if any), express or implied, written or oral.

21 Interpretation

21.1 COMPOSITION

This Agreement comprises these Standard Conditions and the attached Schedules and Special Conditions.

21.2 PRECEDENCE

The Special Conditions and the attached Schedules have precedence over these Standard Conditions to the extent of any inconsistency.

21.3 INTERPRETATION

In this Agreement, unless the context otherwise requires:

- *Agreement* means this Agreement as amended from time to time.
- *Ambush* means the unauthorised association by any person of its name, brands, products or services with the Property or with a party, through marketing or promotional activities or otherwise, whether or not lawful.
- *Competitor* means—in the case of Sponsor:
  - any person who conducts any business which competes (other than incidentally), directly or indirectly, with any business

conducted or services provided by Sponsor or any company related to Sponsor or whose products or services are antithetical to or incompatible with the business, products or services of Sponsor; and
  - any person listed in Schedule 21 or who conducts a business in the industry, or of the nature, described in that Schedule.
- *Competitor* means—in the case of Owner:
  - any person who conducts any event or offers any product substantially similar to the Property anywhere in the Territory or whose operations are antithetical to or incompatible with the Property; or
  - any person or Property listed in Schedule 22 or any Property or event of the nature described in that Schedule.
- *Insolvency* in respect of a party means:
  - the filing of an application for the winding up, whether voluntary or otherwise, or the issuing of a notice summoning a meeting at which it is to be moved a resolution proposing the winding up, of the party;
  - the appointment of a receiver, receiver and manager, administrator, liquidator or provisional liquidator with respect to that party or any of its assets;
  - the assignment by that party in favour of, or composition or arrangement or entering into of a scheme of arrangement (otherwise than for the purposes solely of corporate reconstruction) with, its creditors or any class of its creditors; or
  - a party taking advantage of any insolvency laws to obtain temporary or permanent relief from the payment of its debts or from creditors generally.
- *Media* means any of communication to the public at large, whether by radio, television, newspaper, electronic media (such as the Internet) or otherwise.
- *Owner Benefits* include additional fees or benefits that accrue to Owner by application of the evaluation criteria in Schedule 14.
- *Owner Marks* means Owner's name and trade or service marks, labels, designs, logos, trade names, product identifications, artwork and other symbols, devices, copyright and intellectual property rights directly associated with the Property. If Schedule 16 is completed, the Term is limited to the Owner Marks depicted or listed in that schedule.
- *Sponsor Benefits* may be reduced by application of the evaluation criteria in Schedule 14, and if reduced must be construed accordingly.
- *Sponsor Marks* means Sponsor's name and the marks and other symbols outlined in Schedule 17.
- *Term* includes the period of any option to renew this Agreement if clause 1.5 applies and the option is exercised.

21.4 DEFINED TERMS

Subject to clause 21.3, terms in inverted commas in a Schedule have the meaning outlined in that Schedule.

21.5 CURRENCY

References to currency are to the lawful currency of the country or region of the applicable Law.

21.6 EXAMPLES

Examples given in this Agreement do not limit or qualify the general words to which they relate.

21.7 SIGNATURES

By signing, you indicate acceptance of this Agreement (including the Standard Conditions and the Special Conditions) on behalf of the entity you represent and you declare your ability to sign this Agreement on behalf of the Sponsor/Owner (as the case may be).

Signed for and on behalf of Sponsor by:)
)
)
                                        (signature)

Full name
Title
Witness
Date
SIGNED for and on behalf of Owner by:)
)
)
                                      (signature)

Full name
Title
Witness
Date

Index